12-6

A Book Hunter's Holiday

ADVENTURES WITH BOOKS AND MANUSCRIPTS

THE NATIVITY, PROBABLY BY THE MASTER OF ZWOLLE

A
Book Hunter's Holiday

ADVENTURES WITH BOOKS
AND MANUSCRIPTS

By

A. S. W. ROSENBACH

WITH ILLUSTRATIONS

BOSTON · HOUGHTON MIFFLIN COMPANY · NEW YORK

The Riverside Press Cambridge

1936

The Riverside Press
CAMBRIDGE · MASSACHUSETTS
PRINTED IN THE U.S.A.

TO
THE MEMORY OF
HARRY ELKINS WIDENER

FOREWORD

SIX of the articles in this volume have been published in the *Saturday Evening Post* and I want to express my deep appreciation to Mr. George Horace Lorimer. I wish also to express my grateful thanks for the help received in their preparation from Miss Avery Strakosch.

The chapter on the Libraries of the Presidents has appeared in the *Proceedings of the American Antiquarian Society* (1934). It is a pleasure to acknowledge my indebtedness to Dr. Clarence H. Brigham, the Director of the Society.

Three of the articles are printed here for the first time.

A. S. W. R.

CONTENTS

ILLUSTRATIONS

A Book Hunter's Holiday

ADVENTURES WITH BOOKS AND MANUSCRIPTS

I

LETTERS THAT WE OUGHT TO BURN

ONE summer afternoon about ten years ago, Arnold Bennett and I were taking tea at a charming old place called The Compleat Angler, at Marlow on the Thames. Bennett had selected a table in the garden above the weir, with a broad view of the river. People floated by lazily in punts. The atmosphere was altogether dreamy and delightful. Suddenly we sat up, all eyes. An extremely beautiful woman was drifting close to the shore.

'You know who she is?' We both spoke at once, then smiled. Of course we knew. So did everyone, if the craning of necks at other tables indicated anything. A fascinating American was this lady. Only a short time before, she had made a laughing-stock of one of the most conservative men in England, a certain Lord X, whose real name I am sure you would recognize if I had the temerity to tell it.

Lord X wrote letters to his beautiful friend that were of such an intimate nature that they disclosed a side to his character hitherto entirely unsuspected by his friends. Frankly, they were most amusing even to the casual reader — they were published in the ha'penny press — and I thought them a bit tragic too.

For they revealed what was the passion — his passion
— of a lifetime, and in a manner that fitted neither
his age nor his background.

I looked at Bennett, whose observant eyes were
still on the river.

'What,' I asked, 'do you believe was the first letter
ever written?'

'A dun — or a love-letter,' he replied quickly.

'Which, really?'

'Most likely a dun,' he said in his practical manner,
as he buttered a fresh piece of toast. But I shook my
head, preferring to keep my few illusions. I thought,
and still think, that the first letter ever written was a
love-letter.

It was naturally in my youth that I first became interested in love-letters. Yet, thirty years ago, I had
an altogether different view from that which I have
today. I felt a certain shyness, suffered twinges of
conscience reading letters that were only intended for
the eyes of one person. To me, it was on a par with
peeking through a keyhole. The lines that Shelley
wrote to Mary Godwin, or Keats telling the agony of
his love to 'beautiful and elegant, graceful, silly,
fashionable and strange' Fanny Brawne, seemed to
me sacred. I understood Oscar Wilde's despair, which
caused him to write his exquisite sonnet on the sale at
auction of Keats's love-letters to Fanny Brawne.
Wilde was present that March 2, 1885, little dreaming
that the time would come when his own letters, even
the original manuscript of the poem that he penned

CARL H. PFORZHEIMER

that very day, would appear on the auction block. Wilde's sonnet runs as follows:

ON THE SALE BY AUCTION OF KEATS' LOVE-LETTERS

These are the letters which Endymion wrote
   To one he loved in secret, and apart,
   And now the brawlers of the auction mart
Bargain and bid for each poor blotted note,
Ay! for each separate pulse of passion quote
   The latest price — I think they love not Art
   Who break the crystal of a poet's heart
That small and sickly eyes may glare or gloat.

Is it not said, that many years ago
   In a far Eastern town some soldiers ran
   With torches through the midnight, and began
To wrangle for mean raiment, and to throw
   Dice for the garments of a wretched man,
Not knowing the God's wonder or his woe?

The manuscript of this famous poem I purchased at a sale in New York in 1920. At the same auction, a letter of John Keats to Fanny Brawne sold for eight hundred dollars, and is now in the remarkable collection of my friend Mr. Carl H. Pforzheimer. It was at this sale that Christopher Morley was inspired to write his beautiful sonnet, 'In an Auction Room,' which he dedicated to me and which I consider finer than Wilde's.

In an Auction Room

Letter of John Keats to Fanny Brawne

Anderson Galleries, March 15, 1920, to Dr. A. S. W. Rosenbach

'How about this lot?' said the auctioneer;
   'One hundred, may I say, just for a start?'
Between the plum-red curtains, drawn apart,
A written sheet was held.... And strange to hear
   (Dealer, would I were steadfast as thou art),
The cold quick bids. (Against you in the rear!)
The crimson salon, in a glow more clear,
   Burned bloodlike purple as the poet's heart.

Song that outgrew the singer! Bitter Love
   That broke the proud hot heart it held in thrall,
Poor script, where still those tragic passions move,
   Eight hundred bid: fair warning: the last call:
The soul of Adonais, like a star,
Sold for eight hundred dollars — Doctor R!

                      Christopher Morley

After having acquired the Wilde sonnet for my own collection, I had to have some of the letters that poor Keats penned to Fanny Brawne. My quest had to be most secretive, for my friend, the late Amy Lowell, was then engaged on her great life of Keats. She would have been furious if I had secured letters and refused to surrender them to her. Three finally came my way; one particularly I coveted. Lord Rosebery purchased it at the original sale in 1885 and would never part with it. At his death I bought it from his daughter, Lady Sybil Grant. Written by the poet to Fanny Brawne just before his departure for Rome —

My dearest Girl,

In consequence of our company. I suppose I shall not see you before tomorrow. I am much better to day indeed all I have to complain of is want of strength and a little tightness in the Chest. I envied Sam's walk with you to day; which I will not do again as I may get very tired of envying. I imagine you now setting in your new black dress which I like so much and if I were a little less selfish and more enthousiastic I should run round and surprise you with a knock at the door. I fear

I am too prudent for a dying
kind of Lover. Yet, there is a great
difference between going off in
warm blood like Romeo, and making
one's exit like a frog in a frost
I had nothing particular to say
to day, but not intending that there
shall be any interruption to our
correspondence (which at some future time I propose offering to Murray)
I write something! God bless you
my sweet Love! Illness is a
long lane, but I see you at the
end of it. and shall mend my
pace as well as possible

J - K

KEATS TO FANNY BRAWNE *(continued)*

he died there on February 23, 1821 — he was torn
with jealousy and forebodings:

Wednesday Morn[in]g. [Kentish Town,
towards the end of 1820]

My dearest Girl, I have been a walk this morning
with a book in my hand, but as usual I have been occupied with nothing but you: I wish I could say in
an agreeable manner. I am tormented day and night.
They talk of my going to Italy. 'Tis certain I shall
never recover if I am to be so long separate from you:
yet with all this devotion to you I cannot persuade
myself into any confidence of you. Past experience
connected with the fact of my long separation from
you gives me agonies which are scarcely to be talked
of. When your mother comes I shall be very sudden
and expert in asking her whether you have been to
Mrs. Dilke's, for she might say no to make me easy.
I am literally worn to death, which seems my only
recourse. I cannot forget what has pass'd. What?
nothing with a man of the world, but to me dread-
ful. When you were in the habit of flirting with Brown
you would have left off, could your own heart have
felt one half of one pang mine did. Brown is a good
sort of a Man — he did not know he was doing me to
death by inches. I feel the effect of every one of those
hours in my side now; and for that cause, though he
has done me many services, though I know his love and
friendship for me, though at this moment I should be
without pence were it not for his assistance, I will
never see or speak to him until we are both old men,
if we are to be. I will resent my heart having been
made a football. You will call this madness. I have
heard you say that it was not unpleasant to wait a
few years — you have amusements — your mind is
away — you have not brooded over one idea as I

have, and how should you? You are to me an object intensely desirable — the air I breathe in a room empty of you is unhealthy. I am not the same to you — no — you can wait — you have a thousand activities — you can be happy without me. Any party, anything to fill up the day has been enough. How have you pass'd this month? Whom have you smil'd with? All this may seem savage in me. You do not feel as I do — you do not know what it is to love — one day you may — your time has not come. Ask yourself how many unhappy hours Keats has caused you in Loneliness. For myself I have been a Martyr the whole time, and for this reason I speak; the confession is forc'd from me by the torture. I appeal to you by the blood of that Christ you believe in: Do not write to me if you have done anything this month which it would have pained me to have seen. You may have altered — if you have not — if you still behave in dancing rooms and other societies as I have seen you — I do not want to live — if you have done so I wish this coming night may be my last. I cannot live without you, and not only you but *chaste you; virtuous you.* The Sun rises and sets, the day passes, and you follow the bent of your inclination to a certain extent — you have no conception of the quantity of miserable feeling that passes through me in a day. Be serious! Love is not a plaything — and again do not write unless you can do it with a crystal conscience. I would sooner die for want of you than ———

Yours forever, J. Keats.

Ten years after the Keats sale, during Oscar Wilde's celebrated trial, someone broke into his attractive little house in Tite Street in London, and made away with many of his manuscripts and letters.

By devious routes they appeared at auction or private sale. I remember my brother Philip telling me that directly after the trial, he went into a famous bookshop in London, looking for manuscripts of Oscar Wilde. Although he asked for them in an ordinary tone, the clerk replied in a whisper, and immediately called the proprietor. Sheepishly they led him into a back room, closing the door tightly. To his surprise, he saw on a table the original drafts of Wilde's three plays, 'The Importance of Being Earnest,' 'The Ideal Husband,' and 'Lady Windermere's Fan.'

'Why all this mystery?' exclaimed Philip, now thoroughly astonished.

The bookseller behaved as though the room contained contraband. It was obvious that the sooner he got those manuscripts out of his shop, the better he would feel. So my brother bought them immediately, believing that a man's conduct has nothing to do with his genius.

The papers taken from Tite Street included letters from Constance Lloyd Wilde to Oscar, when she was engaged to him. They are the most heartbreaking letters I have ever read, and bear out my belief that the greatest love-letters are not necessarily written by great people — even, to use Wilde's own phrase, 'lords of language.' Constance Lloyd had no literary pretensions. Here is an extract from one of her letters:

> *My darling Love*, I am sorry I was so silly: you take all my strength away, I have no power to do anything but just love you when you are with me. . . . Every day that I see you, every moment you are with

me I worship you more, my whole life is yours to do
as you will with it, such a poor gift to offer up to you,
but yet all I have and so you will not despise it....
Do believe that I love you most passionately with all
the strength of my heart and mind: anything that you
asked me to do, I would in order to convince you and
make you happy.

... When I have you for my husband, I will hold
you fast with chains of love and devotion so that you
will never leave me, or love any-one as long as I can
love & comfort you.

Today, I do not feel at all squeamish about reading
other persons' love-letters. Of course I refer to those
written by celebrities of the past. As a young man, I
wasn't alone in considering love-letters sacred to the
persons who wrote or received them. Biographers
were very much of that opinion, too. Perhaps that
explains why there were so many dull biographies
published in the early nineteen-hundreds. The truth
is, love-letters show men and women as they really
are. Today, one of the first things an author does, in
planning a biography, is to locate the love-letters
written by the person he is portraying. So, you see,
collecting these letters is a matter of historical interest,
not merely prying into the secret affairs of others.

As I have hinted before, some of the greatest love-
letters were written and are written, not by famous
figures in history and literature, but by people in the
lower walks of life. Take, for instance, those penned
by Edith Thompson to Frederick Bywaters, just before Bywaters murdered her husband in her presence,
and probably with her assistance. She wrote them in

OSCAR WILDE

1921–22, when employed as a bookkeeper in a small millinery shop in London. The letters are terribly sincere, and have a real tragic note. Little did Edith Thompson realize, when on the scaffold in Holloway Prison, that these very letters to her accomplice, which helped to convict her, would some day be given to an inquisitive world, edited, with a preface, by Filson Young.

But the great make better copy, so I shall stick to my last!

Of all the love-letters ever written, I think Napoleon's are the least interesting. Unfortunately, some of the early ones to Josephine are lost. They may have contained at least a flicker of the vital spark, but I doubt it. Eight to Josephine were sold in London in 1933, and brought forty-four hundred pounds. In one, dated March 9, 1796, the month of their marriage, Napoleon wrote with unusual passion:

> You must forgive me, my dear friend, the love with which you inspire me has taken away all my reason; I shall never regain it. My presentments are so terrible that I should be contented if I could see you, press you for two hours against my heart and then die together.

But the letters with which we are familiar, the ones to his second wife, Marie Louise, are typical examples of that quiet emotion which, I understand, all wives resent — just plain colorless affection. Nevertheless, more than three hundred letters to Marie Louise were sold at auction recently in London and were bought by the French Government for fifteen thousand pounds.

Napoleon did write one magnificent letter which I eventually acquired, and which is now in the Pierpont Morgan Library. It has nothing to do with his own grand amours, yet it is a tempestuous one, relating to the first great international romance of this country.

Jerome Bonaparte, brother of the First Consul, was only nineteen when he met, loved, and married the beautiful Betsy Patterson in Baltimore. Napoleon, when apprised of the ceremony, which took place on Christmas Eve, 1803, became terribly enraged, and ruthlessly refused to recognize the marriage. In 1805, Jerome, with his wife, left this country for Spain. Napoleon enlisted the help of his mother, the famous Letizia Bonaparte. Napoleon writes her this remarkable letter:

Madame, Mr. Jerome Bonaparte has arrived at Lisbon with the woman with whom he is living. I have given orders to this prodigal son to return to Milan, by way of Perpignan, Toulouse, Grenoble and Turin. I have written him to understand that if he departs from this route he will be arrested. Miss Paterson with whom he lives has taken the precaution to have her brother with her; I have given orders that she be sent back to America. If she withdraws from the orders that I have given and goes to Bordeaux or to Paris, she will be conducted back to Amsterdam, there to be embarked on the first American vessel. I will treat this young man severely, if in the only interview I shall grant him, he shows himself unworthy of the name he bears, if he persists in wishing to con-

MISS PATTERSON OF BALTIMORE

tinue this liaison, and he is not inclined to wash out the dishonor he has cast upon my name by deserting the flag and his colours for a miserable woman, I will abandon him forever, and perhaps I will make an example [of him] which will prove to young soldiers, to what degree their duty is sacred, and the enormity of the crime which they commit when they desert their flag for a woman. In the supposition that he may return to Milan, write to him, tell him I have been a father to him and that his duty towards me is sacred and that there remains for him, no other salvation but to follow my instructions. Speak to his sister so that she also may write to him, for when I have pronounced sentence I shall be inflexible and his life will be ruined forever.

Your most affectionate son,
NAPOLEON

Au Château de Stupinis,
le 2 floréal an 13 — 22 April, 1805.

The honors Napoleon promised to bestow upon Jerome, together with the aid of their mother, finally brought the young gentleman around, and by decree of the French Senate, his marriage with the 'woman' was annulled. Jerome had evidently none of the backbone of the great Napoleon, or of the determined Letizia, who was a veritable matriarch. Sad to relate, especially in a chapter such as this, Jerome gave up lovely Miss Patterson to marry the plain Princess Catherine of Württemberg. As a reward, he received the title of King of Westphalia. I wonder if Jerome, when in the arms of his consort, did not sometimes think of what he had lost, and whether it was worth while to relinquish a great passion for statecraft.

Of all correspondence, love-letters are the first to be destroyed. The fireplace must have consumed many precious examples that collectors would give their very souls to possess. It is this that makes the chase so interesting. Many that have survived are locked up in old libraries. For instance, the epistles — it is a better name for royal letters — of King Henry VIII to Anne Boleyn are in the Vatican.

How I would like to own the love-letters of Casanova; that would be a real triumph. There is a little cache where the original manuscript of the famous 'Memoirs' remains, together with hundreds of letters from the charming ladies of his intimate circle. If I reveal the place, I am sure someone will forestall me. Yet I will do so, for I like to ruminate upon the fact that Casanova, after his many amatory adventures, settled down as a librarian in the castle of Count Waldstein, at Dux, in Bohemia, where the celebrated 'Memoirs' were written, and where the love-letters now are. There is a rumor, but I cannot vouch for it, that the count considers installing in his ancestral library a cooling system on account of heat generated by the inflammatory contents.

Doctor Samuel Johnson and Mrs. Thrale were a strange pair. Reams of paper have been consumed telling of the most celebrated literary friendship of the eighteenth century. It must be said at the start that Johnson was also the friend of her husband. In fact, when Mr. Thrale stood for Parliament the great lexicographer wrote his speeches for him. Johnson was thus one of the early ghost writers. He also helped him in his brewery business, a rare combination. When Mr. Thrale departed this life, his wife, who never really loved him, and frankly declared before her marriage that Thrale only took her because other ladies refused him, became secretly engaged to Gabriel Piozzi, a handsome Italian musician, whom she first met in 1780. The problem was how to inform Doctor Johnson of the event. He had written her many letters revealing his intense regard for her. After all, Johnson had been her dearest friend and mentor. How could she tell the old man, who was then seventy-three, of her new attachment?

She ended by sending him a circular letter! In this she announced her marriage to Piozzi, with a few explanatory remarks written on the back. Doctor Johnson's reply to Mrs. Thrale is exactly what we would expect of him:

Madam: If I interpret your letter right, you are ignominiously married, if it is yet undone, let us at once talk together. If you have abandoned your children and your religion, God forgive your wickedness; if you have forfeited your Fame, and your country, may your folly do no further mischief.

If the last act is yet to do, I, who have loved you, esteemed you, reverenced you, and served you, I who long thought you the first of humankind, entreat that before your fate is irrevocable, I may once more see you.

I was, I once was Madam
                    most truly yours,
                                SAM: JOHNSON

Fifteen years ago, I set myself a tremendous task which, at first, I never dreamed I could accomplish. I wanted to own the finest collection in the world of 'Rabbie' Burns. To my surprise and delight, it proved to be easier than I thought. Mr. Robert B. Adam, of Buffalo, New York, set me off to a flying start by offering me his wonderful collection, including such treasures as the original manuscripts of 'For a' That and a' That,' 'Tam o' Shanter,' 'Bruce to His Men at Bannockburn,' and more than fifty others. With these in my possession, I was and am constantly on the lookout, not only for manuscripts but for Burns's letters — love-letters.

Burns never made a secret of his attachment for several ladies — Jean Armour, Mrs. M'Lehose (Clarinda), Mrs. Riddell, and Mrs. Dunlop. He immortalized them, as he did everything he touched. The letters he wrote them are amazing. They appear at auction only at rare intervals and fetch a very substantial sum. I paid eight hundred pounds for one of mine. He exposes his soul in them, and yet, with all the intense passion of his being, they exhibit a nobility of character and a chivalrous bearing that were inherent in him. Even in affairs of the heart, Burns was outspoken and fearless. There was nothing of the 'professional' lover in them so frequently found in the amatory correspondence of Lord Byron. I have many of the letters that Burns wrote his fair admirers, but give extracts from only two.

On December 13, 1789, he wrote Mrs. Dunlop concerning his hopes and fears of the future life:

* Wilt thou be my Dearie —
   Tune — Sutor's dochter —

Wilt thou be my Dearie;
When sorrow wrings thy gentle heart,
   Wilt thou let me chear thee! —
By the treasure of my soul!
   And that's the love I bear thee,
I swear & vow, that only thou
   Shalt ever be my Dearie —
Only thou, I swear & vow,
   Shalt ever be my Dearie. —

Jeany, say, thou lo'es me;
   Or if thou wilt na be my ain,
Say na thou'lt refuse me:
   If it winna, canna be,
Thou, for thine, may chuse me;
   Let me, Jeany, quickly die,
Trusting, that thou lo'es me;
Jeany, let me quickly die
Trusting that thou lo'es me. —

                              R. Burns.

ORIGINAL MANUSCRIPT OF ROBERT BURNS'S POEM
'WILT THOU BE MY DEARIE'

Can it be possible that when I resign this frail, feverish being, I shall still find myself in conscious existence! When the last gasp of agony has announced that I am no more to those that knew me & the few who loved me; when the cold, stiffened, unconscious ghastly corse is resigned into earth, to be the prey of unsightly reptiles & to become in time a trodden clod, shall I yet be warm in life, seeing & seen, enjoying & enjoyed?

To Mrs. M'Lehose, the celebrated Clarinda, Burns wrote in a lighter vein under the fanciful name of Sylvander:

I shall certainly be ashamed of thus scrawling whole sheets of incoherence. — The only *unity*, (a sad word with Poet's and Critics!) in my ideas, is Clarinda. There my heart 'reigns and revels.'

What art thou Love! Whence are those charms,
   That dost thou bear'st an universal rule!
For thee the soldier quits his arms,
   The king turns slave, the wise man fool.
In vain we chase thee from the field,
   And with cool thoughts resist thy yoke:
Next tide of blood, Alas! we yield;
   And all those high resolves are broke!

Sᴜʟᴠᴀɴᴅᴇʀ

Burns became an adept at writing love-letters and was so proud of his ability that he frequently wrote them for his friends. The following letter, entirely in his handwriting, is from the original in the possession of that enthusiastic and unregenerate book-lover, my dear friend Mr. Frank J. Hogan:

Madam

What excuse to make for the liberty I am going to assume in this letter, I am utterly at a loss. — I — the most most unfeigned respected for your accomplished worth, if the most ardent attachment, if sincerity & truth — if these on my part will in any degree weigh with you, my apology is these & these alone. — Little as have had the pleasure of your acquaintance, it has been enough to convince me what invaluable happiness must be his, whom you shall honor with your particular regard, & more than enough to inform me how unworthy I am to offer myself a candidate for that partiality. In this kind of trembling hope, Madam, I intend very soon doing myself the honor of waiting on you; persuaded that however little Miss Gordon may be disposed to attend to the suit of a lover so unworthy of her as I am, she is still too good to despise an honest man whose only fault, as to her, is loving her too much for his own peace.

I have the honor to be
MADAM
your most devoted humble servant
Dumfries, March 22, 1785.

The love of Shelley for Mary Godwin has been called everything under the sun. Some say it was ideal; others sordid. Whatever the opinion, it is without doubt one of the great love adventures in literary annals. In 1814, Shelley, after a lurid courtship, decided to throw caution to the winds and ran away with Mary. I had to buy a whole library to obtain the letter Mary wrote to Shelley a few hours before their elopement. Alas! I regret that I have it no longer:

My own Love: I do not know by what compulsion
I am to answer you, but your porter says I must, so
I do. By a miracle I saved your five pounds & I will
bring it. I hope, indeed, oh my loved Shelley, we shall
indeed be happy. I meet you at three and bring heaps
of Skinner street news. Heaven bless my love and
take care of him!

His Own MARY

The elopement caused a veritable sensation.
Mary's father, William Godwin, an improvident
bookseller who had written a treatise on free love, was
heartbroken that his own daughter should have deceived him. To add to his misery, he owed Shelley
money. There is no doubt the alliance spelled tragedy
in his mind. His advocacy of free love must have been
to him a bitter pill. In the following letter to his
friend John Taylor, Godwin graphically described his
wrought-up feelings:

Skinner Street,
Aug. 27, 1814.

Dear Sir: I have a story to tell you of the deepest
melancholy. . . . You are already acquainted with the
name of Shelley, the gentleman who more than
twelve months ago undertook by his own assistance
to rescue me from my pecuniary difficulties. Not to
keep you longer in suspense, he, a married man, has
run away with my daughter. I cannot conceive of an
event of more accumulated horror.

He lodged at an Inn in Fleet Street and took his
meals with me. I had the utmost confidence in him;
I knew him susceptible of the noblest sentiments; he
was a married man, who had lived happily with his
wife for three years. Accordingly the first week of his

visit passed in perfect innocence;... On Sunday,
June 26th, he accompanied Mary, and her sister
Jane Clairmont, to the tomb of Mary's Mother, one
mile distant from London; and there, it seems, the im-
pious idea first occurred to him of seducing her, playing the traitor to me and deserting his wife. On Wednesday, the 6th of July, the transaction of the loan
was completed; and on the evening of that very day
he had the madness to disclose his plans to me, and
to ask my consent. I expostulated with him with all
the energy of which I was master, and with so much
effect that for the moment he promised to give up his
licentious love, and return to virtue. I applied all my
diligence to waken up a sense of honor and natural
affection in the mind of Mary, and I seemed to have
succeeded. They both deceived me. In the night of
the 27th Mary and her sister Jane escaped from my
house; and the next morning when I rose, I found a
letter on my dressing table, informing me what they
had done.

Shelley's own interpretation of love is embodied in
this letter to Mary, written in December, 1816, at the
sober age of twenty-four:

The gratification of the senses soon becomes a
very small part of that profound and complicated
sentiment which we call love. Love, on the contrary,
is a universal thirst for a communion, not merely of
the senses, but of our whole nature, intellectual,
imaginative, and sensitive. He who finds his autotype
enjoys a love perfect and enduring. If men were
properly educated and their natures fully developed,
the discovery of the autotype would be easy...

In 1836 there appeared in London a serial issued in
twenty parts. The work of a hitherto unknown

author, a young law reporter, Charles Dickens, it took the world by storm. It was the case of the man who 'awoke one morning and found himself famous.' This year, 1936, has seen the hundredth anniversary of the publication of the 'Pickwick Papers.' Celebrations in honor of the event have been held in England and in this country by devoted Dickens enthusiasts.

One of the most precious things I have is a portion of the manuscript of the 'Pickwick Papers,' the most valuable Dickens holograph in the world. I recently gave $37,500 to add only five more pages to it. But, of course, this has nothing to do with Dickens's affairs of the heart, except that just before he wrote 'Pickwick,' and preceding his unfortunate marriage to Miss Hogarth, he was in love with Miss Maria Beadnell. It seems Miss Beadnell refused the proposals of Charles Dickens because Henry Winter, an energetic young tradesman, had brighter prospects. I wonder if in after years she regretted it. The world knew — and, of course, this included Mrs. Winter — that Dickens was never happy in his married life. Perhaps she thanked her lucky stars she had rejected him. Who knows?

A true account of Thackeray's love for Mrs. Brookfield has yet to be written, as many of the letters he wrote to her are unpublished. A few have been given to the world, but the real ones, written between 1847 and 1853, in which Thackeray freely unburdens his heart, were in the library of my old friend, Mr. A. Conger Goodyear, of Buffalo, New York, safe from

the prying eyes of biographers. In 1927, Mr. Goodyear decided to sell them at auction in New York, together with Thackeray's correspondence with Miss
Perry and her sister, Mrs. Elliott, to whom he tells
many facts of his romance that he did not dare reveal
to Mrs. Brookfield. These precious memorials of a
great and unselfish love I had to have at all costs, and
I did not consider it too much when I paid $29,500.
They are now in my book vault in New York. To me,
they are far more interesting, more poignant than the
letters written by the Brownings. A hopeless love,
like Thackeray's for Mrs. Brookfield, is far more
dramatic; one moment he is in the clouds, the next
fallen to the bitter earth.

Thackeray made no effort to hide his friendship for
Mrs. Brookfield, and in 1847 he wrote to her:

> But thank God I have never concealed the affec-
> tion I have for you; your husband knows it as well as
> you or I do, and I think I have such a claim to the
> love of both of you as no relationship, however close,
> ought to question or supersede.... As for William
> [Mr. Brookfield], I am bound to him by benefits by
> the most generous confidence and repeated proofs of
> friendship, and to you dear lady by an affection
> which I hope won't finish with my life of which you
> have formed for a long time past one of the greatest
> and I hope the purest pleasures. If I had a bad
> thought towards you I think I could not look my
> friend or you in the face, and I see no shame in owning
> that I love you. I have Wm's. permission, your's,
> that of my own heart and conscience for constantly,
> daily if I can, seeing you. Who has a right to forbid
> me my greatest happiness.

us
45
50

Jan 3.

My dear Lady I like to write you a line to night to show you how I was right about a point w. has been long clear to me, who can understand very well how any man who has been near you and lived or travelled with you must end by what I arrived at years ago, and cannot do otherwise than regard you. When H. Hallam spoke as he did to night I'm sure he said what has been ~~preying~~ upon his mind for many months, & that he was angry at my constant visits to you. But thank God I have never concealed the affection I have for you - your husband knows it as well as you & I do, and ~~you~~ I think I have such a claim to the love of both of you as no relationship, however close, ought to question or supersede. If he ever he asks the question I hope it will frankly be told him that I claim to be as one of your brothers, or the closest and dearest of your friends. As for William, I am bound to him by benefits by the most generous confidence and repeated proofs of friendship; and to you dear lady by an affection w. I hope wont finish with my life of w. you have formed for a long time past the *one of* greatest and I hope the purest pleasures. If I had a bad thought towards you I think I could not look my friend, or you in the face. and I see no shame in owning that I love you. I have w.'s permission, your's, that of my own heart and conscience for constantly, daily if I can, seeing you. Who has a right to forbid me my great happiness? ~~why if the world~~ If neither of these three, who else?. God bless you and us all dear Sister and friend. I like to say So. and declare how much and how entirely I regard you.

WMT.

A REMARKABLE LETTER SHOWING THACKERAY'S INTENSE
LOVE FOR MRS. BROOKFIELD

Again Thackeray wrote to the lady of his heart:

We will love each other while we may here and af-
terwards if you go first you will kneel for me in heaven
and bring me there — if I, I swear the best thought is
to remember that I shall have your love surviving
me and with a constant tenderness blessing my memory. I cant all perish living in your heart. That in
itself is a sort of seal and assurance of heaven. . . . Say
that I die and live yet in the love of my survivors,
Isn't that a warrant of immortality almost? Say that
my 2 dearest friends precede me and enter into God's
futurity spotless and angelical I feel that I have 2
advocates in Heaven & that my love penetrates there
as it were. It seems to me that Love proves God.
By love I believe and am saved.

Many of the letters to Mrs. Brookfield were written
when Thackeray was on a lecture tour in America.
They contain not only expressions of his love but bits
of news. He thus writes to her: 'The prettiest girl in
Philadelphia, poor soul, has read Vanity Fair twelve
times.' I wonder who she was!

Although at first Thackeray states that he was devoted to the husband, William Brookfield, I believe
that later the friendship waned. Thackeray, as was
natural, really began to hate him. The following extract from one of Thackeray's letters in the Perry-
Elliott correspondence is proof. He thus writes to
Miss Perry near the close of the romance:

God bless her. For all the pain and grief to both of
us: I would not have *not* had her love for anything in
the world. It's apart from desire, or jealousy of any
one else, that I think of her and shall always. There
is nothing I know or have ever read or thought of so

lovely as her nature is; the dark spirit is on her poor
husband still I fear. He was not fit to be the mate of
such an angelical creature as that; what a constant
loneliness and grief and rage his life must be — poor
old fellow, it is he who is the most unhappy of us three.

Love-Letters of Famous Americans! What a title
for a book. In colonial days, before the Revolution,
writers seldom preserved such dangerous correspondence, and the love-letters of Washington, Jefferson,
Madison, John Adams, and Alexander Hamilton are
rarely met with. It is said that Martha Washington,
shortly before her death, destroyed nearly all the letters addressed to her by George. A wise woman.
How many secrets have been revealed when packets
of old love-letters, carefully preserved, and tied with
the proverbial blue ribbon, are discovered and published for the delectation of a naughty world.

'I profess myself a votary to love,' Washington
writes in 1758 to Miss Fairfax. He was a surveyor on
his own estate in Virginia, and had many kind neigh-
bors, no doubt. He often went to Alexandria and
Williamsburg on little trips to visit the ladies of his
acquaintance. It is a pity we do not know more of
Washington's early love adventures. When he finally
became engaged to Mrs. Martha Custis, a charming,
rich widow, he gave up all thought of anyone but her,
as the following extract from a letter, unusually frank
for him, written when he was about thirty-three years
old, proves:

Dear Friend Robin: ... my Place of Residence is at
present His Lordship's where I might was my heart

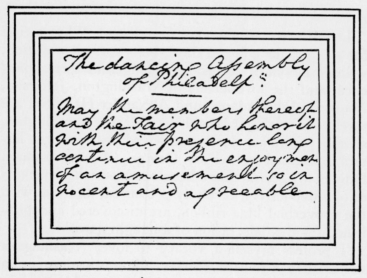

GEORGE WASHINGTON'S TOAST TO THE DANCING ASSEMBLY
OF PHILADELPHIA

disengaged pass my time very pleasantly as there is
a very agreeable Young Lady lives in the same house
[Colonel George Fairfax's wife's sister] but as that's
only adding Fuel to fire it makes me the more uneasy
for by often and unavoidably being in Company with
her revives my former Passion for your Low Land
Beauty where as was I to live more retired from young
women I might in some measure eliviate my sorrows
by burying that chast and troublesome Passion in the
grave of oblivion of eternall forgetfulness for as I am
very well assured that's the only entidote or remedy
that I ever shall be releived by or only recess that
can administer any cure or help to me as I am well
convinced was I ever to attempt anything I should
only get a denial which would be only adding grief
to uneasiness.

In view of the extreme rarity of letters of George to
Martha, I give here one of the few now extant:

July 20, 1758

To Mrs. Martha Custis: We have begun our march
for the Ohio. A courier is starting for Williamsburg,
and I embrace the opportunity to send a few words to
one whose life is now inseparable from mine. Since that
happy hour when we made our pledges to each other,
my thoughts have been continually going to you as
another Self. That an all-powerful Providence may
keep us both in safety is the prayer of your ever faithful and affectionate friend.

Living not far from George Washington in Virginia
was young Thomas Jefferson. I always wanted a love-
letter of Jefferson's, or one relating to his love affairs.
I waited patiently twenty years. Finally, two came
up for sale, together with the greatest letter ever writ-

ten by Jefferson. It was the famous one penned in
Philadelphia on July first, with a postscript written
July 2, 1776. In it he states: 'If any doubt has arisen
as to me, my country will have my political creed in
the form of a "Declaration" which I was lately
directed to draw.' What a thrilling letter for Americans to read! This and the two early amatory ones
were written to William Fleming, a member of the
Committee of the Virginia Convention.

Unable, on November 20, 1930, to attend the sale
myself, I sent my assistant, a namesake of the owner,
John Fleming. I gave him an unlimited bid on the
letters, telling him to phone me the result. 'And be
sure to get the ones about the Virginia ladies,' was my
final admonition.

A few hours later he was breathless on the wire.
'I bought the Jefferson Declaration letter,' he said,
'for twenty-three thousand dollars!'

'Cheap,' I replied. 'It is a great letter! How about
the others?'

'I bought them at a price that will please you.' And
it did.

These letters reveal Jefferson as a rollicking young
fellow with a roving eye. Here is an extract from one
written when he was twenty-one years old:

Richmond [October, 1763]

Dear Will: Last Saturday I left Ned Carters where
I had been happy in other good company, but particularly that of Miss Jenny Taliaferro: and though I
can view the beauties of this world with the most
philosophical indifference, I could not but be sensible

of the justice of the character you had given me of her.
She has in my opinion a great resemblance of Nancy
Wilton, but prettier. I was vastly pleased with her
playing on the spinette and singing, I could not help
to calling to mind those sublime verses of the Cumber-
land genius

> Oh, how I was charmed to be
> Orpheus music all in thee

when you see Patsy Dandridge tell her 'god bless
her,' I do not like the ups and downs of a country
life: today you are frolicking with a fine girl and tomorrow you are moping by yourself. Thank god! I
shall shortly be where my happiness will be less interrupted. I shall salute all the girls below in your
name, particularly S-y P-r. dear Will I have thought
of the cleverest plan of life that can be imagined. You
exchange your land for Edgehill or I mine for Fair-
fields. You marry S-y P-r, I marry R-a B-l. and get a
pole chair and a pair of keen horses, practise the law in
the same courts, and drive about to all the dances in
the country together. . . . I am dear Will

Yours affectionately,

Th. Jefferson

The letters Benjamin Franklin wrote his wife,
Deborah, from the moment he met her until her death
in 1774 are among his most charming. He always relates little bits of news, amusing anecdotes of the
great people he met in France and England during his
many visits. Most of the letters to Deborah are in the
library of the American Philosophical Society in
Philadelphia.

Franklin wrote one letter which some think should
have been burnt, but which has been miraculously

preserved for the delight of posterity. It is his celebrated letter written on June 25, 1745, concerning
'Wives and Old Mistresses.' The original manuscript
came to me in a most curious way. When the Library
of Congress obtained the Franklin Papers from Henry
Stevens in 1882, the letter was strangely missing.
Perhaps Stevens 'held it out' thinking it was too good
a thing to entrust to the American public, and he was
quite right! Stevens finally sold it to a gentleman in
Chicago who left it in his will to an institution in that
chaste city. Chicago, being known for its purity, and
not tolerating anything even slightly indelicate,
offered it to me — at a price, of course, for it did not
hesitate to profit, like a frail sister, from its shame.
I do not give it here, as in this enlightened age, it has
been frequently reprinted.

I once owned a very spirited letter of Franklin's to
a charming young lady, of austere New England,
Miss Kitty Ray.

> *Dear Katy,*
> I left New England slowly & with great Reluctance.
> Short Days Journeys, and loitering Visits on the
> Road, for three or four Weeks, manifested my Un-
> willingness to quit a Country in which I drew my first
> Breath, spent my earliest & most Pleasant Days, and
> had now received so many fresh Marks of the Peo-
> ple's Goodness & Benevolence, in the kind & affec-
> tionate Treatment I had everywhere met with. I
> almost forgot I had a home; till I was more than half-
> way towards it; till I had, one by one, parted with all
> my New England Friends, and was got into the west-
> ern Borders of Connecticut among meer Strangers:

then, like an old Man, who having buried all he lov'd in this World, begins to think of Heaven, I begun to think of & wish for Home; and as I drew nearer, I found the Attraction stronger and stronger, my Diligence and Speed increas'd with my Impatience, I drove on violently, and made such long stretches that a very few Days brought me to my own House, and to the Arms of my good old Wife and Children, where I remain, Thanks to God, at present well and happy.

Persons subject to the Hyp, complain of the North East Wind as increasing their Malady. But since you promis'd to send me Kisses in the Wind, and I find you as good as your Word, 'tis to me the gayest Wind that blows, and gives me the best Spirits. I write this during a N. East Storm of Snow, the greatest we have had this Winter; your Favours come mix'd with the Snowy Fleeces, which are pure as your Virgin Innocence, white as your lovely Bosom — and as cold.

When Franklin arrived in France in 1777 as an emissary of the new republic, he met many charming and distinguished women. He wrote, during his mission to Paris, to his sister Jane Mecom: 'I hope, however, to preserve the regard you mention of the French ladies, for their society and conversation, when I have time to enjoy it, is extremely agreeable.'

One of the chief objects of his visit was to secure a loan from France, which was absolutely necessary if the war with England was to continue. Franklin made several attempts to obtain a grant from the King, without success. He could make no headway with Monsieur Brillon, one of the King's financial advisers. He was at his wits' end. Suddenly a thought came to him, for which he is rightly called our greatest diplomat. He determined to approach Monsieur Brillon through his wife, a beautiful and affectionate woman. When they first met, Franklin was seventy-five; she thirty-six. He was instantly attracted to her. He spoke feelingly of the distress of the struggling colonies, and that if help should not soon be obtained, the war would be lost. Needless to say, it worked like a charm. I purchased, not long ago, the actual receipt given by Franklin to the Treasurer of France for five hundred thousand livres; one of the earliest, if not the earliest, foreign loans made to the United States.

Franklin wrote many extravagant and witty letters from his delightful little house in Passy to his charming neighbor, Madame Brillon. Sometimes he enclosed with them little compositions, such as the 'Story of a Whistle,' which is now a classic. They all contained bits of wisdom in the inimitable manner of Poor Richard. Franklin was proud of them himself. Where were the originals of these exquisite letters to Madame Brillon? I did not know. I had seen copies of some of them, but the whereabouts of the originals was a puzzle. Some years ago, Bernard Faÿ was engaged in writing his life of Franklin. I wrote to him and received no answer. One day he turned up at my office in New York. Yes, he knew. He had discovered them. In an old château in France, in the possession of one of the descendants of Madame Brillon. Through the good offices of M. Faÿ, I finally obtained them. The letters were in beautiful condition,

You see by this time how unjust you are in your Demands and in the open War you declare against me if I do not comply with them. Indeed it is I that have the most Reason to complain My poor little Boy, whom you ought methinks to have cherish'd, instead of being fat and Jolly like those in your elegant Drawings, is meagre and starv'd almost to death for want of the substantial Nourishment which you his Mother inhumanly deny him, and yet would now clip his little Wings to prevent his seeking it elsewhere! —

I fancy we shall neither of us get any thing by this War. and therefore as feeling my self the Weakest, I will do what indeed ought always to be done by the Wisest, be first in making the Propositions for Peace. That a Peace may be lasting, the Articles of the Treaty should be regulated upon the Principles of the most perfect Equity & Reciprocity. In this View I have drawn up & offer the following, viz. —

Article 1.
There shall be eternal Peace, Friendship & Love, between Madame B. and Mr. F. —

Article 2.
In order to maintain the same inviolably. Madᵉ B. on her Part stipulates and agrees, that Mr. F. shall come to her whenever she finds for him...

Art. 3.
That he shall stay with her as long as she pleases.

Art. 4.
That when he is with her, he shall be oblig'd to drink Tea, play Chess, hear Musick, or do any other thing that she requires of him.

Art.

LETTER OF BENJAMIN FRANKLIN TO MADAME BRILLON, PASSY, JULY 27, (1782) — THE FAMOUS 'TREATY' LETTER

Art. 5.

And that he shall love no other Woman but herself.

Art. 6.

And the said M.ʳ F. on his part stipulates and agrees, that he will go away from M. B.ⁿ whenever he pleases.

Art. 7.

That he will stay away as long as he pleases.

Art. 8.

That when he is with her, he will do what he pleases.

Art. 9.

And that he will love any other Woman as far as he finds her amiable. ——

Let me know what you think of these Preliminaries. To me they seem to express the true Meaning and Intention of each Party more plainly than most Treaties. — I shall insist pretty strongly on the eighth Article, tho' without much Hope of your Consent to it; and on the ninth also, tho' I despair of ever finding any other Woman that I could love with equal Tenderness: being ever, my dear dear Friend

Yours most sincerely

B F

FRANKLIN TO MADAME BRILLON (*continued*)

having no doubt been kept with the tenderest care by the lady to whom they were sent.

'Yes, my dear child,' writes Franklin to Madame Brillon, 'I love you as a father, with all my heart. It is true I occasionally suspect my heart of wishing to go farther, but I try to hide that from myself.'

I regret I have space to give only the famous Treaty Letter, written while Franklin was engaged in his great work of drafting the Definitive Treaty between the United States and Great Britain, France and Spain. It is dated from Passy, July 27 (1783):

To Madame Brillon:

What a difference, my dear Friend, between you and me! You find my faults so many as to be innumerable, while I can see but one in you; and perhaps that is the fault of my spectacles. The fault I mean is that of covetousness, by which you would engross all my affection, and permit me none for the other amiable ladies of your country. You seem to imagine that it cannot be divided without being diminish'd. In which you mistake the nature of the thing and forget the situation in which you have plac'd and hold me. You renounce and exclude arbitrarily everything corporal from our Amour, except such a merely civil embrace now and then as you permit to a country cousin...

You see by this time how unjust you are in your demands, and in the open war you declare against me if I do not comply with them. Indeed it is I that have the most reason to complain. My poor little boy, whom you ought methinks to have cherish'd instead of being fat and jolly like those in your elegant Drawings, is meagre and starv'd almost to death for want of the substantial nourishment which you his mother inhumaniy deny him, and yet would now clip his little wings to prevent his seeking it elsewhere!

I fancy we shall neither of us get anything by this war, and therefore as feeling myself the weakest, I will do what indeed ought always to be done by the wisest, be first in making the propositions for peace. That a peace may be lasting, the Articles of the Treaty should be regulated upon the Principles of the most perfect Equity and Reciprocity. In this view I have drawn up & offer the following viz:

Article 1.

There shall be eternal Peace, Friendship & Love, between Madame B and Mr. F.

Article 2.

In order to maintain the same inviolably Made. B. on her part stipulates and agrees, that Mr. F. shall come to her whenever she sends for him.

Article 3.

That he shall stay with her as long as she pleases.

Article 4.

That when he is with her, he shall be oblig'd to drink tea, play Chess, hear Musick, or do any other thing that she requires of him.

Article 5.

And that he shall love no other woman but herself.

Article 6.

And that said Mr. F. on his part stipulates and agrees that he will go away from Madame B's whenever he pleases.

Article 7.
That he will stay away as long as he pleases.

Article 8.
That when he is with her he will do what he pleases.

Article 9.
And that he will love any other woman so far as he finds her amiable.

Let me know what you think of these Preliminaries. To me they seem to express the true meaning and Intention of each party more plainly than most treaties. I shall insist pretty strongly on the eighth Article, tho' I despair of ever finding any other woman that I could love with equal tenderness; being ever, my dear dear friend

Yours most sincerely,

B. F.

Love-letters of Abraham Lincoln are practically unobtainable. To find an authentic one is a real achievement. Because there are so few, the clever forger has taken advantage of our common frailty, supplying enthusiastic but gullible collectors with ardent Lincoln letters addressed to his early loves, Ann Rutledge and Mary Owens. People are constantly bringing me their 'Lincoln' letters, and it is incredible how many persons who should know better are taken in. The letters are time-stained, for forgers can age paper as quickly as distillers can age their spirits. Experts, too, have been fooled. But here is a real one. Not exactly a passionate love-letter but a romantic one, a mock petition, written in a facetious mood from Springfield in 1839, when he was thirty. It is signed by Lincoln and three of his friends, and addressed to Mrs. Orville Browning. It runs:

> *To the Honorable Mrs. Browning:* We, the undersigned, respectfully represent to your Honoress, that we are in great need of your society in the town of Springfield and therefore humbly pray that your Honoress will repair forthwith to the seat of Government bringing in your train all ladies in general who may be at your command and all Mrs. Browning's sisters in particular and as faithful and dutiful petitioners we promise that if you grant this our request, we will render unto your Honoress due attention and faithful obedience to your orders in general and to Miss Browning's in particular.
>
> In tender consideration whereof we pray your Honoress to grant your humble petitioners their above request and such other and further relief in the premises as to your Honoress may seem right and proper; and your petitioners as in duty bound will ever pray, etc.
>
> A. Lincoln
> O. B. Webb
> (Signed) J. J. Hardin
> John Dawson

Lincoln's love — if you care to call it that — for Mary Owens began in 1836. She must have been, from the brief accounts we have of her, an attractive, intelligent woman. Lincoln deeply admired her, and in a short time proposed. He wrote her some of the strangest love-letters ever penned by man. They are filled with local political gossip and reasons why she should not marry him! Reading between the lines, one comes to the conclusion that in them Lincoln tried to be scrupulously honest and fair, even to sacrificing his own happiness for the woman to whom he was so devoted. Lincoln knew he was no Adonis, and he knew also that he could never endow her with worldly goods. He states so plainly in his letter — too plainly. According to the Lover's Code, 600th Revised Edition, Article 987, Chapter XXIV, Page 9911, which he evidently never studied, the mistake Lincoln made was to put his shortcomings into print. He was his own devil's advocate — a dangerous thing in wooing. After reading the following letter, written by Lincoln to Miss Owens from Springfield on May 7, 1837, you can hardly blame the fair recipient for not encouraging the young lawyer's attentions. Perhaps she could not read between the lines:

Friend Mary: I am often thinking of what we said about your coming to live at Springfield. I am afraid you would not be satisfied. There is a great deal of flourishing about in carriages here, which it would be your doom to see without sharing it. You would have to be poor, without the means of hiding your poverty. Do you believe you could bear that patiently? Whatever woman may cast her lot with mine, should any ever do so, it is my intention to do all in my power to make her happy and contented; and there is nothing I can imagine that would make me more unhappy than to fail in the effort. I know I should be much happier with you than the way I am, provided I saw no signs of discontent in you. What you have said to me may have been in the way of jest, or I may have misunderstood it. If so, then let it be forgotten; if otherwise, I much wish you would think seriously before you decide. What I have said I will most positively abide by, provided you wish it. My opinion is that you had better not do it. You have not been accustomed to hardship, and it may be more severe than you now imagine. I know you are capable of thinking correctly on any subject, and if you deliberate maturely upon this before you decide, then I am willing to abide your decision.

What Lincoln evidently needed was a lover's lexicon.

Not everyone in the colonies, like Franklin and Jefferson, could spontaneously put his emotions onto paper. Thousands had to rely on the poetic fancies of others.

In the early days in America, almost every bookseller had on his shelves what were called 'Ready Letter Writers.' The printing presses turned them out by thousands. They contained letters on every conceivable subject, and for every occasion. All you had to do was to copy one that pleased you and send it over your own signature. I inherited one of these quaint compendiums, which was issued in Philadelphia in 1793:

THE AMERICAN LETTER-WRITER:

Containing, a Variety of Letters on the most common Occasions in Life, Viz: Friendship, Duty, Advice, Business, Amusement, Love, Marriage, Courtship, &c. . . . to which are Prefixed, Directions for Writing Letters, and the Proper Forms of Address

Judging from the timeworn covers, it must have been frequently used by members of my family.

VALENTINE WRITTEN BY EDGAR ALLAN POE

These little books are still published, and book-sellers tell me they have a ready sale. This reminds me of an interesting story.

Some years ago I had the pleasure of meeting a lady of unusual grace and brilliancy. She was a book-collector. To me, that was her greatest charm. One day I showed her my little volume on the art of letter-writing. Instantly her usual calm expression changed and her eyes took on a startled look.

'Of all the women in the world,' she said, 'why did you bring it to me?'

She then told me her story.

'I was eighteen years old,' she said, 'when a young man for whom I did not particularly care asked me to marry him. He kept repeating his proposal; my parents were on his side, for he was energetic and am-bitious. I, however, did not love him, and constantly refused his offers. One morning I received a letter. I knew the handwriting, and reluctantly opened it. It was one of the most beautiful letters I had ever read, filled with tender sentiment and the most im-passioned expressions of his love. There was so much fire in it, so much burning desire that the letter seemed to scorch my fingers. Yet I wondered how a man of his cold exterior could have written such a letter. Had I misjudged him? I showed the letter to my parents — girls did that in the nineties — and they assured me that only a fellow of exceptional worth could write like that. So, I married him.

'We lived together for nearly twenty years. One day, looking through an old trunk, I found a worn book with a slip of paper marking a page. I opened it and had the shock of my life.

'Of course, you know the rest of the story! That letter, so tender and passionate, the letter that had caused me to marry him, my husband had copied out of that very volume. I had discovered it years too late. As I come of a generation that considers a contract a contract, I could not walk out of my husband's life because of a counterfeit love-letter. My advice to you is,' she said in parting, 'never keep an old love-letter; it may prove a boomerang.'

'Better still,' I rejoined, 'never write one.'

In the language of the poet:

> Lives of great men all remind us,
> As these pages o'er we turn,
> That we're apt to leave behind us
> Letters that we ought to burn.

II

OLD MYSTERY BOOKS

THE earliest mystery stories, or the tales that described the lives of contemporary criminals, made the same human appeal in their day as do our modern thrillers. The rarest old books are those describing the lives of great criminals. Few of these volumes remain, because, as in the case of the children's books of a later period, they were literally read to tatters. It is a pity that these bloodcurdling mementoes of a former age are not more eagerly sought after by collectors; they should have a strong appeal for the book-lover. Reports of old trials, for instance, that still vibrate with life as the characters in them try to elude death; the last dying speeches, too, of famous criminals, dramatically flung upon the breeze that played about the scaffold; and the moving narratives of actual murders! These are the real foundation, the source materials for the plots of many of the greatest dramas, romances, novels, and mystery stories of English literature. The modern detective story can be traced directly to them.

Fifteenth-century readers enjoyed the thrill of a good murder story as avidly as you and I. Perhaps more so. The blackguards who peopled those early stories were a thousand times more picturesque in

their badness than the businesslike, unromantic criminals of today. Surely the swashbucklers and the
pirates, the vagabonds and cozeners, and the many
other exotic types to whom murder was all in the day's
work — or play, for that matter — as they swept
ruthlessly through the fifteenth and sixteenth centuries, were more emotionally disturbing, and satisfying, too, than those fellows who abound now in their
natty, pinch-waisted suits behind a machine-gun.

One of the earliest works, if not the earliest, concerning celebrated criminals is a little volume published at Nuremberg by Peter Wagner about 1488,
called 'Dracole.' When first I began to form my collection around this fascinating subject of criminals
and their ilk, I was most eager to have a copy of this
quaint volume. The truth was, I had never seen it.
Naturally I went first to the British Museum when
in London in search of it. But alas, it was not there!
I was told that a copy had been brought to light,
about that time, in an old monastic library in Ger-
many. It was discovered hidden among papers in the
desk of an old monk, the librarian. How often, I wonder, had he fired his imagination with its horrible contents when it was supposed that he studied his breviary!

I hurried to Berlin. 'Dracole' was not there. The
German dealers had never heard of it. A few days
later, at luncheon in the Hotel Adlon, and about one
hour before my departure, I mentioned the work to a
noted collector. He startled me by saying he had seen

TREASURE ROOM AT 15 EAST 51ST STREET, NEW YORK

a volume containing this tract but had no idea what
had become of it. I was in a fever now to secure what
I believed to be, necessarily, the very foundation of
my collection. I began to do a bit of detective work
myself. Wherever I went on the Continent, I made a
tour of the book marts, asking questions here, there,
and everywhere. It seemed to me that there was a
peculiar, almost mysterious ignorance concerning
'Dracole's' whereabouts.

Exactly one week after my return to this country,
the volume was safe in my library. A European bookseller had beaten me to it. He had arrived in Ger-
many a few days before me, secured 'Dracole,' then
sworn his dealer to silence. A joke on me, which only
I realized. Yet it whetted my appetite to such an extent that I paid an inordinate price to possess it, but
not so much as I would have if my friend, the dealer,
had known of my long quest and desire for it. I read
this old volume over and over. It fascinates me with
its deeds of depredation, and gives me that delightful
chamber-of-horrors sensation, as I sit in my library,
my eyes glued to its pages, deaf to approaching dawn
and the milk wagon. At such a time I live the daring,
fearless existence of the fifteenth century while my
blood runs cold at the story of the atrocious deeds
committed from 1456 to 1464 by that notorious tyrant, Dracole Waida!

This ancient 'Dracole' contains the earliest known
portrait of a celebrated criminal. A woodcut, colored
by hand, an expressive picture, shows a bust of
Dracole with his long black locks and heavy mus-

tachios. Topping the dark head is an elaborate, high-crowned hat ornamented with a large brooch. The locale of this fifteenth-century despot is the same as that of the nineteenth-century vampire, Dracula, made famous by Mr. Bram Stoker. Whether the creator of the latter thriller was aware of the existence of the former, I do not know.

So far as crime is concerned, no age has produced more finished villains than that of Shakespeare. Murders, especially the premeditated ones, with all sorts of vivid detail — as attractive to read now as the day they were written — were committed with a regularity that gave a romantic color and an exciting uncertainty to everyday life. In a way the grim tragedy of murder supplied all the tense interest that we seek in the modern detective mystery. The Elizabethan audience was quick to applaud the triumph of virtue and the resultant death of the villain. Writers, then as now, eagerly pounced upon real-life stories that dealt with the machinery of murder.

Imagine Shakespeare searching through the musty accounts of a murder case in order to find plots for his plays. Arden of Feversham, first published in 1592, attributed to Shakespeare by Swinburne, has for its theme an actual murder committed a few years before the dramatist's birth.

In 1551, Thomas Arden, a private gentleman living at Feversham, in the county of Kent, was brutally murdered at the instigation of his wife, Alice. Here was a great sensation whose echoes were heard the length and breadth of the kingdom.

DRACOLE WAIDA

Earliest known printed picture of a criminal (1488)

Master Arden's demise was arranged not only by the faithless Mistress Alice and her worthless paramour, one Mosbie, but by several accomplices as well. It was an open secret in the Arden household that the master's presence, no longer desired, must be terminated. Mistress Arden, having already failed in an attempt to poison her husband, was unsure of herself. A gentleman of the road, roistering Black Will, a fellow who accented his every other word with an oath, was therefore engaged for ten pounds to do the actual killing. Several times Black Will tried to get his man along the country highways, but without success. Master Arden was changeable, and at the last moment would decide not to ride along the route where Black Will lay in wait for him; or else he was unexpectedly accompanied by friends upon his journeys. Most murderers would have become discouraged. Finally Black Will and a partner, one Shakbag, hid in a closet in the poor fellow's own house and attacked him at a prearranged moment. When he had breathed his last, Alice stepped forward and stabbed him several times in the chest, to make assurance doubly sure!

The unknown author, possibly Shakespeare, took this somber tale and rewrote it, without missing a single macabre detail. No one recognized better than he the perennially popular appeal of a murder story, especially a true one. The title-page is enough to excite the curiosity of the most jaded reader of any time:

The Lamentable and True Tragedie of M. Arden of Feuersham in Kent. Who was most wickedlye murdered, by the meanes of his disloyall and wanton wyfe, who for the love she bare one Mosbie, hyred two desperat ruffins Blackwill and Shakbag, to kill him. Wherein is shewed the great mallice and discimulation of a wicked woman, the vnsatiable desire of filthie lust and the shamefull end of all murderers.

Shakespeare wisely made all that he could — what author has made more? — out of murder and violent death. Witness his first published play, 'Titus Andronicus,' 1594, of which there is but one surviving copy, in the remarkable Henry C. Folger collection in Washington. In this there are eighteen characters, thirteen of whom are killed, six at the hands of one man alone! In 'Romeo and Juliet,' 1597, three murders and two suicides take place. In 'Macbeth,' written about 1605, six of the main characters are killed and one turns to suicide. In 'King Lear,' 1608, six more are murdered, with another suicide and a natural death to boot. 'Pericles,' 1609, has four violent deaths, and in 'Othello,' issued in 1622, but performed much earlier, a mere three persons are killed, touched off with another natural death as well as a suicide. In the most famous tragedy of all, 'Hamlet,' the father of the character from whom the play takes its name is done away with, even before the actors have stepped upon the boards. Seven others are killed outright during the ensuing acts, with a drowning to end Ophelia's troubles. Altogether there is a satisfying total of nine deaths! Fifty-one persons die in seven plays! Would any modern dare to parallel this record?

Vado mori fogiatis:alios concludere noui: fortiu viroz est magis morte cotenere vita odisse:
Coclusit breuiter mozs michi:vado mori. Stultu est timere: quod vitari non potest.

Omnia mozs tollit doctu ceadisse cathone:Atqz ipsum socratem procubuisse ferunt.

Mozs

Et vos regens in achademia
Qui plurimos coegistis studentes
Nichil prodest dicere epa
Vestras decet dimittere artes
Vestri certe nigrescant dentes
Studete nunc prout deus soluit
Dimittite grammatice partes
Mozs hominem subito dissoluit

Magister scole

Sciencia vero gramatica
Aliarum est introductio
Iuuenibus autem ppotheca
Et artium vera discaudo
Sinc illa nullum conspicio
Ad maiora vlla peragere
Sed ecce nunc morte deficio
In omnibus decet inapere

Mozs

Super equum atqz cursarium
Vos armiger nunqz ascendetis
Mozs arripit nunc vestru brauium
Aspicite quid huc facietis
Mundum vero statim dimittetis
Non expedit lanceam currere
Vt ego sum ita vos eritis
Quis contra me potest resistere

Armiger

Heu non vite habeo spacium
Quia morti decet obedire
Nunc dimitto regis seruicium
Et cum illa compelloz nunc ire
Ad pristinum non possum redire
Huc tam pie sum conductus modo
Sicuti mozs cogit me abire
Mori decet nescimus quando

6 i

'THE DANCE OF DEATH,' PARIS, 1490

Shakespeare had a noble predecessor in this line of work. Thomas Kyd in 'The Spanish Tragedy' anticipated all that Shakespeare accomplished, but without his finesse. Here Hieronimo, the hero, tries to avenge the murder of his son, Horatio, almost in the manner of Shakespeare's Prince Hamlet. 'The Spanish Tragedy' was probably the most popular of all plays of that lusty era. No less than thirteen editions appeared before 1633. Not a single copy of the first edition, 1592, has been left to us. There is a precious example, however, of the second issue, which may be seen in the British Museum.

When Shakespeare wrote in 'Henry IV':

> Rob, murder, and commit
> The oldest sins the newest kind of ways,

he probably had Kyd in mind, or perhaps the latest inventions of the Italian romance writers. But these lines should be an admonition to mystery writers of all times. They form a perfect credo for the modern fellows.

There were no newspapers in those days to supply readers with such lurid tales as the full-blooded Elizabethans craved, so they fairly devoured every murder play as it came off the press. There has never been such a demand for the printed play before or since. Today, no matter how successful a play is, very few copies of it are sold. But then, when a sensational murder was committed, the pamphleteers got busy and issued booklets which described every detail of the tragedy. Indeed, our ocher-colored journals had nothing on these little chapbooks. Quickly they were snapped up in Saint Paul's Churchyard or in the Fleet. In the Bodleian Library there is a unique copy of one of these pamphlets, dated 1605. In it is an account of

> Two most unnaturall and bloodie Murthers. The one by Maister Caverley, a Yorkshire Gentleman, practised upon his wife, and Committed upon his two Children, the three and twentie of Aprill 1605.
>
> The other by Mistris Browne, and her servant Peter, upon her husband, who were executed in Lent last past at Bury, in Suffolke, 1605.

Although the second murder was as gory a domestic tragedy as you would care to read about, it was the first story in the volume which caught the public taste and took hold of the imagination of a contemporary writer. The murderer, Caverley, a man of good family, had for years dissipated his married life and his fortune. When his wife gently suggested she might help him to get out of the financial and other difficulties that were about to swamp him, the trouble started. His reply was neither short nor sweet, and although the pamphleteer could hardly have been on the spot at its utterance he reported it freely. Caverley said frankly to his wife:

> Base strumpet! [whom thogh I maried I never loved] shall my pleasure be confined by your wil? If you ... be in want, either beg, or retire to your friends, my humor shal have the auntient scope. Thy rings and jewels I wil sel, and as voluntarie spend them as when I was in the best of my estate.

AN
EXCELLENT
conceited Tragedie
OF
Romeo and Iuliet,

As it hath been often (with great applause)
plaid publiquely, by the right Honourable the L. of *Hunsdon*
his Seruants.

LONDON,
Printed by Iohn Danter.
1597

TITLE-PAGE OF FIRST EDITION OF 'ROMEO AND JULIET,' 1597

So began the tragic end of the Caverley family, which later inspired a popular drama brought out as 'A Yorkshire Tragedy.' Like 'Arden of Feversham,' this play has been attributed to Shakespeare, but it is now placed among his doubtful works.

The stories of actual crime are more interesting, as a rule, than the most brilliant imaginative writing. The great writers from Shakespeare to the present day knew this, and frequently based their works upon actual crimes. The mind of a murderer is always a fascinating study, and naturally receives great attention because it makes excellent copy. The primitive man used every method to escape detection that is known to the modern killer. Ephraim Avery, Troppmann, Neil Cream, William Palmer, Doctor Crippen, and Landru, all celebrated criminals of the nineteenth and early twentieth centuries, were no more success-ful in their efforts to prevent detection than their predecessors of an earlier age.

The English dramatists of the sixteenth and seven-teenth centuries often lifted their plots from contem-porary Italian romances, but there is no record of an actual murderer following their example when con-templating his crime. Although the Elizabethan au-thors frequently used English translations of Italian storybooks, such as Painter's 'Palace of Pleasure,' and admired the Italians' cold, detached method of nar-rating a crime, the murderers of Old England dis-dained such foreign aid. They created their own backgrounds and did not take kindly to imported ways. Nor do our own criminals put into practical execution the fantastic devices employed throughout the alluring novels of Agatha Christie, Phillips Oppenheim, S. S. Van Dine, G. K. Chesterton, and Edgar Wallace. The cases where an actual murderer has followed the plot in a novel are decidedly rare. Such fellows work out, in their own devious minds, the best and easiest way. And certainly, when you read the literature of roguery, the early tracts that deal with actual crimes, it is easy to understand why no writer, not even Edgar Allan Poe himself, has created plots more daring or more brilliant in execution than those crimes which actually took place four or five centuries ago.

Poisoning in the fifteenth century was considered a fine art. The noble Borgias were its greatest exponents, but I don't know of any early English criminal who copied their methods. I have an autograph letter addressed to the Gonfalonier of Florence from the noted Cesare Borgia, who probably murdered his brother, Giovanni, Duke of Gandia. Unfortunately, it does not mention his famous poison ring, with which he is supposed to have annihilated many of his enemies.

The story of the noble Venetian gentleman who wished to put out of the way another noble Venetian gentleman must appeal to all bibliophiles. Knowing his friend to be a book-lover, the first gentleman had a colorless poison placed most deftly upon the leaves of a lovely old manuscript, probably the tales of Boccaccio. When the book-lover turned the pages, which were stuck together at a critical point in the story, he touched the tips of his fingers to his lips to moisten them, and the next second was upon the library floor in his dying agony! Such stories are extremely interesting but not practical.

The subject grows in absorbing interest. In the period of Shakespeare the authors themselves, as if to give their works more reality, frequently took part in crimes. Ben Jonson, the great contemporary of Shakespeare and a fellow actor, killed Gabriel Spencer in 1598, and was sentenced to prison for manslaughter, but was later reprieved. He has the distinction of being one of the few literary men branded for a crime. Christopher Marlowe, one of the sweetest lyrical poets of any age, and a famous dramatist, was also the associate of cutpurses and thieves. Of his assassination in 1593, when but twenty-nine, a brief account is given by Meres in his 'Palladis Tamia,' 1598, as follows:

> As the poet Lycophron was stabd to death by a certaine rival of his; so Christopher Marlow was stabd to death by a bawdy serving-man, a rivall of his in his lewde love.

Little wonder there is such color in these old plays and poems! And no one has written about the writers of this bewitching era with a livelier pen than Charles Lamb, who, with De Quincey, was an intimate associate of the celebrated poisoner, Thomas Griffiths Wainewright. When comparing our own times with the more piquant age of Shakespeare, the bands of adventurers that included brutish, masterless men, disbanded soldiers and other vagrants must not be forgotten. They infested the city and countryside and had to have their leaders, quite like the crooks of to-day. How surprisingly alike are the methods of the underworld in all ages!

I searched for years to obtain a little volume that gives a priceless account of the London underworld. Unfortunately, I did not find it in the approved manner — unknown and unsought by others, upon the shelf of a dingy bookstore. Oh, no! I ran across it in the library of an astute collector who well knew its worth! I finally secured it at a king's — or a gangster's — ransom! It is entitled:

> A Caveat or Warening for common cursetors vul-garly called Vagabones by Thomas Harman, and sold by the publisher William Griffith, at his shop in St. Dunstan's Churchyard in 1567.

Only three other copies are known. I consider my-self lucky to have mine. It is a book no crime library should be without, and I have often thought old Har-man's advice particularly applicable to us who are in the throes of gang warfare today. He desires all con-stables and bailiffs ruthlessly to set aside all fear, sloth and pity, in order that the 'rascal rabblement,' as he quaintly puts it, may no longer ravage the country. He gives all details of the canting crews, their various rackets, and in what line they are most expert. Who was this Thomas Harman who had such intimate knowledge of the brotherhood of vagabonds? No one knows, but you can feel the ring of truth in his every word. Here is an unforgettable picture of the seamy side of life of that period, painted in true colors.

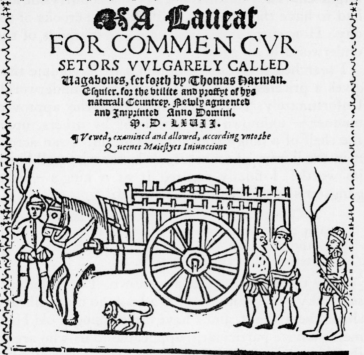

A Caueat
FOR COMMEN CVR
SETORS VVLGARELY CALLED
Uagabones, set forth by Thomas Harman.
Esquier. for the vtilite and proffyt of hys
naturall Countrey. Newly agmented
and Imprinted Anno Domini.
M. D. LXVII.

¶ Vewed, examined and allowed, according vnto the
Queenes Maiestyes Iniunctions

IMPRINTED
at London in Fletestret at the signe of the
Faulcon by Wylliam Gryffith and are to be
solde at his shoppe in Saynt Dunstones
Churche yarde. in the West.

'A CAVEAT FOR COMMEN CURSETORS,' BY THOMAS HARMAN
(ABOUT 1567)

Another link with the past is the use of fantastic names or descriptive titles which attach themselves to star gang leaders and other criminals. The journalists of today are no more apt at devising them than were the pamphleteers of an earlier, a wiser and a more creative time. We have much to learn from the Golden Age of English letters. If Gyp the Blood and Leftie Louie are names that stir our curiosity, how about Moll Cutpurse, the Roaring Girl, Dick Devil-Barn, Grand Catchpole, and Captain Pouch? The flamboyant Roaring Girl, immortalized in Middleton's comedy, was an actual person, Mary Frith, who really ruled a vast fraternity of criminals in London. A sort of queen of the roisterers. No 'bobbed-haired bandit' has even approached famous Moll Cutpurse, who could draw a dagger or wield a rapier as expertly as any of her bootlicking henchmen.

If such little volumes as Harman's are rare, the early novels dealing with the day-by-day lives of rogues and cutthroats are even more so. In the wake of the Renaissance it was the Spaniards who originated this kind of fiction. The famous story of 'Celestina,' by Fernando de Rojas, first issued in 1499, should be in every library of roguery. But alas! The first edition exists in but a single copy. It was originally in the library of Mr. J. P. Morgan, who, with characteristic generosity, presented it to Mr. Archer M. Huntington, who in turn gave it to the Hispanic Society of America in New York City which he had founded. The 'Celestina' is the rather grim recital of the hot passion of Calisto, a 'young, enamoured

Gentleman,' for the beautiful Meliboea, who at first rejects him. Calisto is assisted in his quest by the wily old bawd, Celestina, one of the most terrible and realistic figures in all fiction. After the stereotyped stories of the Italian authors this was a marked innovation. The story is told with all the pitiless frankness of the modern novelist. It took Europe by storm.

The strangest part of all is that the 'Celestina' served as the source of the first regular English play. An adaptation by John Rastell, entitled 'A New Comedy in English, wherein is described as well the Beauty and Good Properties of Women as their Vices,' appeared in London about 1525. It was popularly called 'Calisto and Meliboea.' Like its Spanish predecessor, it exists in a solitary example.

Now, by rights, this unique volume should be in my crime library. When I was a student in the English Department of the University of Pennsylvania under my beloved teacher, Doctor Felix E. Schelling, I made the discovery that the 'new comedy' of 'Calisto and Meliboea' was the earliest regular English play. The earlier writers on the subject had always mentioned 'Ralph Roister Doister,' by Nicholas Udall, as the first 'regular' play in the English language. All the textbooks had it as such. The 'Celestina,' put into English clothes in the early years of the sixteenth century, was the first to suppress the allegory and abstract quality of the old morality plays, and the earliest to employ customary Christian names for its characters. And so the romance of roguery is responsible for our first comedy! I have been able to secure noble treasures from English libraries, but this one is, I fear, beyond me. It is safely locked up in the Malone collection in the Bodleian Library at Oxford. I made a special pilgrimage a few years ago to see it and had to be content to hold it for a few moments in my hands. How I envied Raffles! And in my own library I am compelled to be satisfied with the translation by James Mabbe, issued in 1631, which is as common as blackberries.

How strange that the first complete record of low life, and the greatest story of its kind, came from the pen of Don Diego Hurtado de Mendoza, in whose veins flowed the bluest blood of Spain! His 'Lazarillo de Tormes,' written and published 1554, during Mendoza's student days, was an instant and everlasting success, being read today with as much enjoyment as it was almost four hundred years ago. The *picaro*, the knowing rogue who narrates his misdeeds with his tongue in his cheek, who is a past master of cheating and hypocrisy, who retains his devil-may-care attitude and a sharp sense of humor always, claims a universal audience. Mendoza hardly appreciated the importance of his work, but Rouland did and turned the pleasant history of 'Lazarillo de Tormes' into English in 1586. Its artistic realism, smacking of the soil, again made its success instantaneous, and the *picaro* thrived anew in England. But the first editions of these charming tales of ancient rogues, while not as rare as hens' teeth, are practically unprocurable. One must be satisfied with later ones.

It is of extraordinary interest that just as the greatest of dramas dealt with rapine and assassination, so the first English novel should also have for its hero a most splendid rascal. Shakespeare was right, as usual, when he said, 'Murder, though it have no tongue, will speak with most miraculous organ.' To obtain a sixteenth-century edition of the earliest English historical romance is worthy of the mettle of the most astute collector. Of the first edition of Thomas Nash's 'the Unfortunate Traveler, or the Life of Jack Wilton,' issued in 1594, not half a dozen copies remain today. It was read to pieces, not so much for its excellence as for its matter, for it deals with an unscrupulous rascal who stopped at nothing. With horrors aplenty, its detailed realism makes your blood congeal, as cold shudders run up and down your spine. Ghost stories are not in it with Nash's famous descriptions. The Elizabethans wanted their horrors laid on thick and plenty, and Nash was equal to the task. His account of the execution of Cutwolfe is graphic, to say the least, and I shall give you but a taste to whet your appetite:

> At the first chop with his wood-knife woulde he fish for a man's heart, and fetch it out as easily as a plum from the bottome of a porredge pot. He woulde cracke neckes as fast as a cooke crackes egges: a fidler cannot turne his pin so soone as he would turne a man of the ladder: brauely did he drum on this Cutwolfes bones, not breaking them outright, but like a sadler knocking in of tackes, iarring on them quaueringly with his hammer a great while together.

But it was not only in the Bodleian Library that I wanted to be the Raffles of Mr. E. W. Hornung's romances. I remember one summer when I decided to get away from books for a time and put my mind upon less serious things. My doctor had said it would be good for me. I went to Canada.

On the way back, driving through the beautiful Connecticut Valley, I chanced to notice a name upon a signpost. It seemed quite familiar, although I could not recall having toured that particular part of New England before. Then it came to me.

About six months before I had met a very charming young man. I will call him Brown. Brown had urged me to visit him. We had parted with my promise that if ever I were in his neighborhood I would stop in. He had, he said modestly, a nice little library, half of which he had inherited, and half of which he had picked up, as he put it, himself. Here I was now passing through his village.

Stopping at the local store, I telephoned him. He seemed delighted, but explained that he would have to be away for an hour or more. Would I mind waiting for him at his home?

'Mr. Brown will return shortly,' the butler told me upon my arrival, 'and he would like you to make yourself at home in his library.'

I doubt if I have ever seen a more disorderly book room! Books of all sizes and all values, everywhere! Heaps of them upon the long seventeenth-century Spanish table by which I sat; piles of them on the floor, on the window sills of the tightly closed windows. Heavy, large volumes weighing down small, slender, delicately bound ones.

I was amazed. How did young Brown ever find anything?

Suddenly I stopped. Across the library, upon a shelf among a few loosely placed, slanting volumes, something attracted my eye. I could see no title — nothing. But I knew — I knew what that book was, although I myself had not placed it there. It was the first edition of Thomas Hellier — the first single volume dealing with wholesale murder in Colonial America. And I had searched over eighteen years here and abroad for this little work!

I put my hand to my face. It was damp with perspiration, excitement — and a peculiar sense of fear. Then, as though invisible accusing eyes were upon me, I walked casually but cautiously to the shelves. First I carelessly picked up a volume to the left of it, and another to the right. And then, with my heart pounding, I removed this remarkable bit of Americana.

Now like a miser I ran my fingers over the precious leaves and drank in the title page. I read:

> The vain prodigal life, and tragical penitent death of Thomas Hellier born at Whitchurch near Lyme in Dorsetshire: who for murdering his Master, Mistress, and a Maid, was executed according to Law at Westover in Charles City, in the Country of Virginia, neer the Plantation called Hard Labour, where he perpetrated the said Murders. He suffer'd on Munday, the 5th of August, 1678, and was hanged up in chains at Windmill-Point on James River. London, 1680.

THE
Vain Prodigal LIFE,
AND
Tragical Penitent DEATH
OF

Thomas Hellier

Born at *Whitchurch* near *Lyme*
in *DORSET-SHIRE:*

Who for Murdering his Master,
Mistress, and a Maid, was Executed according to Law at *Westover* in *Charles* City, in
the Country of *Virginia*, neer the Plantation
called *Hard Labour*, where he perpetrated
the said Murders:

He Suffer'd on Munday the 5th of *August*, 1678.
And was after Hanged up in Chains at *Windmill-
Point* on *James River.*

Exemplum sicut Speculum, Exempla docent.

Examples on Record have ever stood
T'instruct the after-Ages, (bad or good.)
For, each Fxample is a Looking-glass,
In which we may behold (each man his face.)

LONDON:
Printed for *Sam. Crouch*, at the Princes Arms, a corner-shop of
Popes-head-alley in *Cornhil.* 1680.

TITLE-PAGE OF THE LIFE OF THOMAS HELLIER,
LONDON, 1680

What a terrible temptation was mine! This young book-lover, who had a wild, queer gift for obtaining great books — did he even know that he possessed this volume? How could he, in all that confusion — a confusion of years? If I did accidentally take it, who would suspect me? And even so, who would think to accuse me? For a few moments my mind worked in and out of channels as slippery as any criminal's.

I stood up now and returned the coveted little book to its dusty shelf. As I did so, my sleeve knocked an octavo volume to the floor. I picked it up, opened it as a sort of outlet for the mental torture I had passed through a few moments before. It was the first volume of Harrison Ainsworth's 'Jack Sheppard,' and on the title-page I read this quotation from one of the greatest picaresque novels, 'The Life and Actions of Guzmán D'Alfarache':

> 'Upon my word, friend,' said I, 'You have almost made me long to try what a robber I should make.'

I left Brown's library that day with a heavy heart, but Thomas Hellier wasn't in my pocket — acquired honestly or otherwise. My host did not force it upon me, as one book-lover to another, as he saw me gloat over it. He said, 'Choice bit, eh?' and that was an end to it.

But like all book-collectors, Brown had a queer streak, and with surprise one day I learned a part of his library was to go upon the auction block. How my fingers trembled as I looked through the sale catalogue! Thomas Hellier was there! Today it is one of the prizes of my crime library both as to rarity and the price I paid for it!

I think that the autograph letters of great criminals and manuscripts of celebrated stories dealing with this charming subject are even more interesting than the printed volumes. They are almost unprocurable. For instance, there is, I believe, only one autographed letter known of Robert Catesby, the chief contriver of the Gunpowder Plot, who was killed after the plot was discovered.

This letter is addressed 'to His Lovinge Cosin, Mr. John Grant.' It should be in some great library in England, but I simply must keep it in my collection, where it nestles with the letters of cutthroats, murderers, assassins, and thieves.

The autographs of these old birds are rarer than that of Button Gwinnett. The signer of the Declaration of Independence from Georgia could at least write, but most of these early rascals could not even sign their names. Hence the extreme scarcity of their autographs.

I can never hope to secure manuscripts of the 'Celestina' or the other crime masterpieces of the fifteenth or sixteenth century. I have been lucky enough, however, to obtain manuscripts of a later period which I have not touched upon in this article. Henry Fielding on 'Murder,' Ainsworth's 'Jack Sheppard,' and the first draft of Stevenson's novel, 'Doctor Jekyll and Mr. Hyde,' and Conan Doyle's 'Sherlock Holmes.' Who would want more?

BOOK ROOM IN NEW YORK

III

THE TRAIL OF SCARLET

NOT long ago I dined in a fashionable restaurant on Park Avenue. At the next table sat a famous — or should I say infamous? — gunman. Savile Row had done its best for him, but the disguise was weak. A gentleman famous in world affairs was also present, yet the chief attention of the diners was concentrated upon this notorious fellow. I learned from the head waiter that it wasn't unusual for the ladies who came there to ask to meet him, and that débutantes lost interest in their expensive food and collegiate escorts whenever he appeared.

With an historical bump rather highly developed, I could not help thinking of the time in the eighteenth century when the same attention was given to highwaymen, pirates, and smugglers. Hero-worship of blackguards was as rampant then as now. Such men as Jack Sheppard, the housebreaker; Jonathan Wild, director in a corps of thieves; and other *chevaliers d'industrie*, like Dick Turpin, were the heroes of dozens of stories, and were directly responsible for three or four of the finest novels in the English language.

Hangmen were as celebrated as their lawful victims, and their appearance 'in person' near the gibbet at a popular hanging brought as many cheers and boos from the crowd as a presidential candidate does today. There was John Price, known down the years as Jack Ketch, 'a rogue and a liar who was not believed when he spoke the Truth.' He achieved his great ambition to become the common hangman of London. You can imagine the delight of the criminal classes when Price himself was eventually hanged for murdering a woman in May, 1718.

Henry Fielding was a committing magistrate, and many of London's underworld came before him. A gentleman, Fielding called the yearly three hundred pounds salary he received 'the dirtiest money upon earth.' Shortly before he died, he published and distributed a curious little pamphlet that gives a living account of 'providential detections of murderers.'

In my everlasting chase after books that treat of the fascinating subject of crime and criminals, I was lucky enough to secure the original manuscript of Fielding's 'Of Outlawry in Criminal Causes.' The creator of Tom Jones speaks scathingly of 'a new kind of drunkenness . . . by that poison called gin.' I was very happy when I had a chance to bid in this manuscript, even though my friend, Mr. Owen D. Young, sat not far from me, a hapless loser. The sixty-seven hundred dollars I had to pay for it was a bit of a strain on my pocketbook, but I solaced myself with the thought of the rarity of Fielding manuscripts, especially on a subject in which I was so much interested.

I remember once going into an English 'pub' where

Chapt. 1. Of Outlawry in Criminal Causes.

THE ORIGINAL MANUSCRIPT OF FIELDING'S 'OF OUTLAWRY
IN CRIMINAL CAUSES'

the man behind the bar, a large florid fellow in a tight white apron, winked at me. Thinking at first that I had imagined this familiarity, I took no notice. Then he winked again, and leaned over the bar anxiously toward me.

'You are Doctor Rosenbach, aren't you?' he asked. 'The doorman at the Carlton knows you. He's a friend of mine. I asked him all about you, ever since the time my missus read you had bought "Alice in Wonderland." She's been dotty about old books ever since. Paws through them whenever she can. Now she's found something for you, sir!'

I wasn't exactly surprised. For years all sorts of people have brought old books to me, have stopped me on the streets and in hotel lobbies. Although ninety-nine out of one hundred may be valueless the hundredth book may prove a treasure. I've made it a rule to look at any book which is directed my way. After all, didn't a plasterer once surprise me with a fine copy of Poe's 'Tamerlane'?

The bartender now opened a closet door behind him. From it he took a small flat package wrapped in newspaper, laid it upon the bar, and tore off the wrapper rather excitedly. Immediately I recognized the volume, a nice copy in excellent condition of Henry Fielding's treatise, 'An Enquiry Into the Causes of the late Increase of Robbers,' which he blamed on gin. I bought it on the spot!

People believed in the eighteenth century, exactly as they do today, that alcohol was responsible for much of the evil of the world. And the present 'alky' racket had nothing on the 'schnapps' one of the olden days. The running of the product of the juniper berry from Holland to London was filled with thrills and dangers.

The gin traffic stirred London first in the early part of the eighteenth century. King William's men are said to have seduced the working people with it; ever since they have had a goodly thirst for 'the 'orrid stuff.' But gin-drinking threatened to ruin the lower classes, and even worse, the brewers! I own a contemporary report, a warning which recounts with horror that good English beer was being avoided like poison! Naturally, the sensitive people in authority preached against the gin-shop, which flourished like the green bay tree all over London. Smollett, who seemed to know, declared a man could get quite pleasantly squiffed on a penny, and dead drunk on tuppence!

To cast out the new evil, the Volsteads of that day drew up regulations which prohibited the gin-shop, or palace, as it was more often called. The gin-drinkers went literally wild. Troops were ordered out to try to quiet thirsty crowds, but in vain. It was then that the 'blind pig' was born, the disreputable ancestor of our speak-easy. And instead of calling gin 'gin,' it answered to such names as 'Sangree,' 'Ladies' Delight,' or 'Cuckold's Comfort.'

Jack Sheppard continued to be a hero for a century and more after his execution at Tyburn in 1724. In 1839, William Harrison Ainsworth, Dickens's great friend, made him the hero of 'Jack Sheppard, a

[44.]

Chapter VI.

The Murder on the ~~Oldern~~ Thames.

Mr. Wood, as we have already ~~seen, was dragged to the first pump~~, and ~~reared~~ to a sound ducking. All the mud and filth he had picked up in the road was speedily washed off. But soiled clothes would have been a luxury in comparison with the drenching he now endured. Like Clearly, he thought that "a fish must have a cursed life of it," and felt assured "that he should have such an aversion to water after this, that he offered scarce ever be cleanly enough to wash his face again." As a last stroke of malice, his mouth was forced open, and he was compelled, at the risk of suffocation, to swallow above a gallon of the ~~stained~~ obnoxious fluid. His wig, saturated with moisture, was then ~~clapped~~ placed upon his ~~head~~; and his hat, turned inside out, was clapped upon the wig. In this lamentable plight he was ~~kicked out~~ of the debris's garrison.

Congratulating himself, that, if he had had a dip upon his ~~body~~ ~~it was still~~ ~~dry carpenter,~~ as soon as he was liberated, ~~set off at full speed; and~~ hurrying he scarce knew whither, (for there was such a continual buzzing in his ears, and dancing in his eyes, as almost to take away the power of reflection,) he held on at a brisk pace, till his ~~breath~~ and strength completely failed him.

On ~~coming to himself~~ regaining his breath, he began to consider whither chance had led him; and, rubbing his eyes to clear his sight, he perceived a sombre pile ~~and~~ with a lofty, ~~new~~ tower and broad roof, immediately in front of him. This structure at once satisfied him as to where he stood. He knew it to be Saint Saviour's Church. As he looked up at the massive tower, the clock tolled forth the hour of midnight. The solemn strokes were immediately answered by a multitude of chimes sounding across the ~~Thames~~ Thames, amongst which the deep note of ~~the~~ Saint Paul's was plainly distinguishable. A feeling of inexplicable awe crept over —— turn on ——

MANUSCRIPT OF 'JACK SHEPPARD' BY WILLIAM HARRISON
AINSWORTH

Romance,' which is probably the best-known of his works. I have the original manuscript of this long-winded novel. Jack lived a short, merry career which ended on the gallows in his twenty-third year, and yet Ainsworth makes three stout volumes out of it. Although the account of Eugene Aram was issued in the eighteenth century in a slim pamphlet, Bulwer Lytton made a lengthy novel from these meager details which he published in three volumes in 1832.

The end of the eighteenth and the beginning of the nineteenth century witnessed the decline of the narrative style of fiction dealing wholly with criminals and their triumphs. Instead of the great galaxy of red-blooded rogues that inspired the mid-century writers, a new school developed which concentrated upon the supernatural — ghosts and specters. Such tales of terror as 'The Monk,' written by Matthew Gregory Lewis when he was nineteen, and 'The Mysteries of Udolpho,' by Mrs. Ann Radcliffe, with all the machinery of the supernatural, ousted the more virile, true-to-life stories upon which the public had gorged for so long in the novels of Fielding and Smollett.

Only two writers in the English language have actually changed the course of literary history in the realm of detective fiction — Edgar Allan Poe and Sir Arthur Conan Doyle. The detective stories of the Victorian period were really elegant romances, but with little analysis and subtlety. I have never cared particularly for 'The Moonstone' of Wilkie Collins, even though it has had hosts of friends since it was issued in 1868. I, however, have profound respect for its hero, Sergeant Cuff, one of the greatest detectives created by any author. I prefer 'The Woman in White.' Count Fosco, in this work, has been truly called the 'spiritual parent of scores of subtly humorous, sardonic villains.' The inception of the story is said to have come to Wilkie Collins quite out of the air. Late one night in the fifties, he and his brother Charles accompanied a friend through the dimly lit, semi-rural roads and lanes of North London. They were walking along, the story goes, chatting gaily in the summer night, when suddenly they heard a piercing scream, a woman's voice. Almost immediately a garden gate near by opened and a woman, very beautiful in the moonlight, dressed in white, came toward them. When she saw the three men, she paused, then darted past them down the shadowed road. Wilkie Collins dashed after her and, he later said, learned her strange story from her own lips.

Speaking of this important feminine character reminds me that no writer has ever created a really brilliant woman detective. Wilkie Collins did make the attempt; once in 'No Name,' and again in 'The Law and the Lady.' Although women often prove clever associates in the detective agencies of real life, and use their wiles to lure criminals, they seldom have the pure deductive minds which in fiction, or out of it, characterize the great detectives.

Thackeray, a true student of the eighteenth century, tried to imitate the classical mystery writers of

A CORNER OF DOCTOR ROSENBACH'S AMERICANA LIBRARY

that time in his shorter stories, such as 'Catherine' and 'Barry Lyndon.' According to his notebook, he based the latter on a character from Chambellan's history, 'L'Empire; ou Dix Ans sous Napoléon Premier,' published in 1836. 'Catherine' was founded on the career of a murderess named Catherine Hayes. Thackeray, playing the part of literary crusader, vainly hoped by this work to counteract the practice of making ruffians and harlots the prominent characters in fiction. In 1850, when 'Pendennis' appeared in serial form, another Catherine Hayes, an Irish prima donna, happened to be in the limelight. Thackeray, his mind on the murderess, had probably never heard of the singer. When he chanced to couple the name of the former with that of the latter, the Irish press grew furious. He had to suppress the passage. This is interesting, because it interprets the initial letter which Thackeray drew for the fifteenth chapter of the second volume of 'Pendennis,' which, while humorous, must seem to the average reader otherwise meaningless.

I am the fortunate owner of an original manuscript of an unpublished story by Thackeray. It deals with Bluebeard, the world's best-known murderer after Cain. This monster appealed strongly to Thackeray, and a more whimsical piece of fiction never came from his pen. Not long after this acquisition, seven pen-and-ink sketches were drawn to me as to a magnet, and I became the proud possessor of Thackeray's fantastic depiction of Bluebeard's love affair with Fatima!

Dickens had a gift for portraying horror which paralleled his humor. His severer critics accuse him of turning men into monsters of the one type or the other. In 'Bleak House,' I feel sure he was quite unconscious of creating one of the finest detectives of all time. Mr. Bucket, the detective officer, as Dickens called him, is surely one of the great personalities in detective fiction. I doubt that the character of Lady Dedlock, in the same story, has ever been surpassed in fiction, and certainly the lawyer, Mr. Tulkinghorn, is marvelously true to life. This brings up the fact that lawyers, like ministers, are rarely, if ever, the heroes of novels. They are generally shown as stealing the last farthing of spinsters, widows, and orphans. A friend of mine, defender of several famous criminals — who, incidentally, takes a busman's holiday reading detective stories when he's working upon a difficult case — said to me earnestly: 'My business is to improve mankind. I try to turn murder into manslaughter, and adultery into felonious gallantry!'

Dickens was always interested in ferreting out strange murder mysteries. He used to prowl about the London streets alone, or with Wilkie Collins, in a frantic search for material. In Paris they wandered together, their eyes open, their imaginations sensitive to each peculiar-looking person or thing. Once, Collins relates, he and Dickens came upon an old bookshop there, where they found some dilapidated volumes and records of French crime — a sort of French Newgate Calendar. Dickens exclaimed excitedly: 'Here is a prize!'

Bluebeard & Butts at a breakfast table. Talbot waiting

Talbot   My lady's brother and Captain Jones my lord
       Took breakfast early and went out to hunt.

Bluebeard   What horses had they Talbot?
Talbot   please your lordship
       The Trumpeter came down with Captain Jones

Butts   Confound it! he was worth two hundred pound
       The Trumpeter, if he was worth a _guinea_ sixte.
       And never up to Captain Jones's weight
       What call had he, the great big hulking beast,
       To ride a lady's horse and break his knees?

Bluebeard.   Wont you try this grilled Salmon Butts?

Butts.   the thin, please.

Talbot   And Mundy took the black horse, and bay. Bolter
       For Mr. Shacabac, to Marley Woods
       Last night my lord the meets at Marley Wood
       I'm gente drove over on the Trap with Higgs
       And please my lord if I might be so bold
       To speak before Mr Butts

Bluebeard   Speak everything
       Jack Butts is like myself at Bluebeard Castle
Butts   You're very good
Bluebeard   the fish is very good.
       Speak Talbot — what's the matter?

Talbot   please my lord
       The keepers boy is here with a black eye
       Wt Captain Shacabac has been wapping of him ..

Bluebeard   Suppose that Captain Shacabac was a preacher
       And gave the keepers varlet a black eye
       The keepers varlet would be proud of his eye —
       let him assess the value of his bruise
       and count it in his wages.

Talbot   Please my lord

MANUSCRIPT OF 'BLUEBEARD'
BY W. M. THACKERAY

Wholesale murder fascinated Charles Dickens. I own his copy of 'Narratives of Remarkable Criminal Trials,' which was translated from the German in 1846 by Lady Duff-Gordon. It contains detailed, revolting accounts of forty or fifty murders committed by that evil genius, the nurse, Anna Maria Zwanziger, the German Brinvilliers. She evidently took a certain pleasure in watching her patients die. In case they didn't succumb by natural means, she hurried them over the void. This harpy continued her career for many years before her crimes were discovered, and she paid the penalty.

Dickens's signature is sprawled in large letters on the title-page of this book. He presented this copy to James T. Fields, February 24, 1868, when he was in Boston. No doubt he and Wilkie Collins gloated over these mystery narratives together.

One of the greatest books from Dickens's pen deals with a murderer's career — 'The Mystery of Edwin Drood,' which Longfellow considered one of his most beautiful works. It was left incomplete. He was working on it the afternoon before his death, June 8, 1870. Perhaps it is just as well that the ending of this immortal story will never be revealed. Here is a mystery within a mystery, and the solution was only within the tremendous brain of Charles Dickens. Thousands of suggestions have been made, but the real dénouement remains a mystery. Like nearly all Dickens's works, this book was to be issued in twenty parts. Only six were ever published by his old publishers, Chapman & Hall, in 1870. We do know from the author's letters, and from what he told his friend and biographer, John Forster, that the novel was to consist of the murderer's own view of his crime and the causes that led up to it. I rejoice in the autograph manuscripts of the 'Pickwick Papers' and 'Nicholas Nickleby,' but alas! the original draft of 'Edwin Drood' will never be mine. This unfinished manuscript is one of the prized possessions of the Forster collection in the South Kensington Museum in London. Dickens was to receive $37,500 for the copyright, and a half share of the profits after the sale of twenty-five thousand copies, as well as five thousand dollars for advance sheets to be sent to America. This totaled the largest sum ever paid, up to that date, by a publisher for a novel. I would gladly have given that much for this last manuscript of Charles Dickens.

Strangely enough, the publishers, with publishers' unerring instinct, had inserted a clause in their agreement with Dickens for certain arrangements in case of his death. He was hardly cold before attempts were made to evolve the mystery; 'John Jasper's Secret,' a sequel to 'Edwin Drood,' appeared in London in eight parts and ran from October, 1871, to May, 1872. Many writers of small reputation have written other 'sequels' and second parts to this work.

What a pity it is that Edgar Allan Poe was not alive to solve this riddle! He had already tried his hand very successfully at that sort of thing. On May 1, 1841, in Graham's weekly, the *Saturday Evening Post*, appearing in a new and enlarged form, Poe gave distinction to the number by an analogous

ORIGINAL DRAWING OF BLUEBEARD BY W. M. THACKERAY

exercise of his analytical powers when he exposed the plot of Dickens's 'Barnaby Rudge.' When Dickens learned that Poe had seen only the material afforded by the introductory chapters, he was so surprised he wrote to ask him if he were the devil!

Poe's favorite and guiding quotation was from the celebrated sentence in Sir Thomas Browne's 'Urn Burial,' which runs:

> What song the Syrens sang, or what name Achilles assumed when he hid himself among women, although puzzling questions, are not beyond *all* conjecture.

About twenty years ago a middle-aged man came into my office in Philadelphia, with a soiled pamphlet, which had no wrappers or other indication on the outside of what was contained within. I bought it for the proverbial song. It was none other than the first issue of a story that was to influence detective-story writing for all time, 'The Murders in the Rue Morgue,' by Edgar Allan Poe. The original wrappers, lacking in this copy, bore the title, 'Prose Romances Number 1, containing "The Murders in the Rue Morgue" and "The Man that Was Used Up." Philadelphia, William Graham, 1843.' Only seven or eight copies of this precious pamphlet are known. The expression, 'worth its weight in gold,' is more than applicable to this little pamphlet of forty pages. Although it was published at twelve and a half cents, in 1909 Mr. Pierpont Morgan paid thirty-eight hundred dollars for the copy now in his library; within the last three years a copy found in a bundle of pamphlets in New York City sold privately for twenty thousand dollars!

The original manuscript of 'The Murders in the Rue Morgue' had many hazardous adventures before it reached its final and permanent resting-place. Its hairbreadth escapes are worthy of the pen of Poe himself. It was rescued in 1841 by J. W. Johnston from a waste-basket in the office of Barrett & Thrasher, Printers, No. 33 Carter's Alley, Philadelphia, where he was serving as an apprentice. According to his account, *Graham's Magazine*, in whose pages the story first appeared, was printed in the aforesaid office and the revised proof read in the *Saturday Evening Post* office, Chestnut Street above Third, within a door or two of the old *Public Ledger* building. After the story had been put in type and the proof read, the manuscript found its way into the waste-basket. Johnston picked it from the basket, asked and obtained leave to keep it, and took it to the residence of his father, with whom he then boarded.

Mr. Johnston was a maker of daguerreotypes, and he relates that twice in 1850 when almost all his books, papers, pictures, and apparatus were consumed by fire, the Poe manuscript, folded within the leaves of an old music-book, escaped destruction. Again, in 1857, the manuscript was in danger of the flames, but was miraculously preserved from all injury except a slight discoloration.

Johnston served in the Civil War from 1861 to 1864, and, on leaving to join the colors, again lost sight of the old music-book in which he had left the manuscript.

In 1869, Johnston consigned a great deal of rubbish to the ashpile, the old music-book sharing the fate of other worthless articles. 'My next-door neighbor,' Mr. Johnston states, 'thinking it had been inadvertently thrown away, picked it from the ashpile and handed it to me. On opening the book, I again beheld the much-neglected and long-mislaid manuscript!'

Finally, in 1881, having resolved not again to subject it to unnecessary risks, Johnston sold it to George W. Childs, the famous publisher and editor of the *Public Ledger*, who presented it to the Drexel Institute in Philadelphia, where today it may be viewed by all admirers of Edgar Allan Poe. Childs paid only a few dollars for it. I would give my eye-teeth to own it! Today it is priceless! I own, however, the copy of Poe's 'Tales of the Grotesque and Arabesque' which he presented to his wife, Virginia, and another, thoroughly annotated by him, with a new title in manuscript, 'Phantasy Pieces.'

Poe intended issuing his series of mystery tales in parts, as Dickens did. The first, 'The Murders in the Rue Morgue,' was the only one so to appear. Two years later, 1845, Wiley & Putnam issued them under the mere title, 'Tales, by Edgar Allan Poe.' This is the greatest volume of short stories ever to appear from the hand of man. It contained, in addition to 'The Murders in the Rue Morgue,' 'The Mystery of Marie Rogêt,' 'The Purloined Letter,' 'The Black

Cat,' 'The Gold-Bug,' and seven others. Poe had been accused of plagiarism a few years before this volume appeared. My uncle, Moses Polock, in whose bookshop in Philadelphia Poe spent much time, often told me that all the publishers were afraid to deal with Poe because in 1839 he had put over 'The Conchologist's First Book' on the publishing house of Haswell, Barrington & Haswell, which he had stolen — or, to use a gentler word, 'borrowed' — from a book by Thomas Brown, published in Edinburgh four years before. At the same time, Poe was continually accusing his literary enemies of plagiarism, whilst being guilty himself. However, in 'Tales' he redeemed himself as only a divinely gifted writer could. Here's an originality, actually a new method, invented by him, which has been used as a model by writers of mysteries ever since. Although he used newspaper accounts, as in 'The Mystery of Marie Rogêt,' for his plots, the manner of his telling is entirely novel. This story was based upon an actual happening. A young woman, Mary Cecelia Rogers, was found murdered near New York. Poe merely changed the locale to Paris. When his story appeared, this particular murder case was fresh in the mind of every inhabitant of the Eastern seaboard, with the public clamoring, as usual, for more of the actual details. In a letter of Poe's in my possession, he states:

> Nothing was omitted in Marie Rogêt but what I omitted myself. All that is mystification. The story was originally published in Snowden's Lady's Com-

cising an author you must imitate him, ape him, out-Herod Herod. She is grossly dishonest. She abuses Lowell, for example, (the best of our poets, perhaps) on account of a personal quarrel with him. She has omitted all mention of me for the same reason — although, a short time before the issue of her book, she praised me highly in the Tribune. I enclose you her criticism that you may judge for yourself. She praised "Witchcraft" because Mathews (who toadies her) wrote it. In a word, she is an ill-tempered and very inconsistent old maid — avoid her.

7 — Nothing was omitted in "Marie Rogêt" but what I omitted myself: — all that is mystification. The story was originally published in Snowden's "Lady's Companion". The "naval officer" who committed the murder (or rather the accidental death arising from an attempt at abortion) confessed it; and the whole matter is now well understood — but, for the sake of relatives, this is a topic on which I must not speak further 8 — "The Gold Bug" was originally sent to Graham but he not liking it, I got him to take some critical papers instead, and sent it to The Dollar Newspaper which had offered £100 for the best story. It obtained the premium and made a great noise 9 — The "necessities" were pecuniary ones. I referred to a sneer at my poverty on the part of the Mirror 10 — You say — "Can you hint to me what was the terrible evil" which caused the irregularities so profoundly lamented?" Yes, I can do more than hint This evil" was the greatest which can befall a man. Six years ago, a wife, whom I loved as no man ever loved before, ruptured a blood-vessel in singing Her life was despaired of I took leave of her forever & underwent all the agonies of her death She recovered partially and I again hoped. At the end of a year the vessel broke again — I went through precisely the same scene Again in about a year afterward. Then again — again — again & even once again at varying intervals Each time I felt all the agonies of her death — and at each accession of the disorder I loved her more dearly & clung to her life with more desperate pertinacity But I am constitutionally sensitive — nervous in a very unusual degree I became insane, with long intervals of horrible sanity During these fits of absolute unconsciousness I drank, God only knows how often or how much As a matter of course, my enemies referred the insanity to the drink rather than the drink to the insanity. I had indeed, nearly abandoned all hope of a permanent cure when I found one in the death of my wife. This I can & do endure as becomes a man — it was the horrible never-ending oscillation between hope & despair which I could not longer have endured without total loss of reason. In the death of what was my life, then, I receive a new but — oh God! how melancholy an existence!

And now, having replied to all your queries let me refer to The Stylus. I am resolved to be my own publisher. To be controlled is to be ruined. My ambition is great. If I succeed, I put myself (within 2 years) in possession of a fortune & infinitely more. My plan is to go through the South & West & endeavor to interest my friends so as to commence with a list of at least 500 subscribers. With this list I can take the matter into my own hands. There are some few of my friends who have sufficient confidence in me to advance their subscriptions — but at all events succeed I will. Can you or will you help me? I have room to say no more.

Truly Yours — E A Poe.

THE FINEST LETTER WRITTEN BY EDGAR ALLAN POE — RELATES TO 'MARIE ROGÊT' AND 'THE GOLD BUG'

panion. The naval officer who committed the murder (or rather the accidental death arising from an attempt at abortion) confessed it; and the whole matter is now well understood — but for the sake of relatives this is a topic on which I must not speak further.

Poor Poe has been accused of going even to Herodotus for the plot of 'The Murders in the Rue Morgue,' but this is as much fiction as any of his own stories! He might have read somewhere similar plots, but it was the freshness of his interpretation that made them so vital and enchanting. The manner in which he unraveled the mystery in 'The Purloined Letter' approaches the unique in literature. I believe these stories of Poe will live when 'The Raven' and 'Annabel Lee' and some of his other poems are forgotten.

Poe's mind was analytical to an uncanny degree. It was clinical too. I think his early works on cryptograms had a great deal to do with his success in unraveling mysteries. And it is probable that he received a certain vicarious pleasure in writing these superb stories which dealt with subtle analysis. He analyzed himself with that same critical retrospection he used in his fiction. I have a letter in his hauntingly beautiful handwriting dated January 4, 1848, which is partly unpublished. In it he shows clearly this terrific tearing himself apart. It is his own explanation of what the early writers consider the greatest blemish upon Poe's character. Here it is:

> You say — Can you *hint* to me what was the terrible evil which caused the irregularities so pro-

foundly lamented? Yes; I can do more than hint.
This 'evil' was the greatest which can befall a man.
Six years ago, a wife, whom I loved as no man ever
loved before, ruptured a blood-vessel in singing.
Her life was despaired of. I took leave of her forever
& underwent all the agonies of her death. She recovered partially and I again hoped. At the end of a
year the vessel broke again — I went through precisely the same scene. Again in about a year afterward. Then again — again — again — & even once
again at varying intervals. Each time I felt all the
agonies of her death — and at each accession of the
disorder I loved her more dearly & clung to her life
with more desperate pertinacity. But I am constitutionally sensitive — nervous in a very unusual
degree. I became insane, with long intervals of horrible sanity. During these fits of absolute unconsciousness I drank, God only knows how often or how
much. As a matter of course, my enemies referred
the insanity to the drink rather than the drink to the
insanity. I had indeed, nearly abandoned all hope of
a permanent cure when I found one in the *death* of
my wife. This I can & do endure as becomes a man —
it was the horrible never-ending oscillation between
hope & despair which I could *not* longer have endured without total loss of reason. In the death of
what was my life, then, I receive a new but — oh
God! how melancholy an existence!

If a man could write in this madly beautiful strain
of himself, is it any wonder that he could apply such a
gift so well to his stories?

The greatest detective in all fiction was the creation
of the brilliant mind of Edgar Allan Poe — C. Auguste Dupin, of 33 rue Donat, Faubourg Saint-Ger-

main, Paris. He was the first scientific detective. Although a creature of Poe's imagination, he is more alive today than any detective who has ever existed, not excepting Eugène François Vidocq, principal agent of the French police until the year 1827, or our own Pinkerton. Dupin was the hero of three marvelous stories: 'The Murders in the Rue Morgue,' 'The Mystery of Marie Rogêt,' and 'The Purloined Letter.'

We are fortunate enough to have Poe's own opinion of his famous 'Tales' in an unpublished manuscript in my possession. Poe, like Walt Whitman, sometimes 'puffed' his own books in anonymous reviews or those signed with a fictitious name. In 'A Reviewer Reviewed' he takes eight pages to give his own views of his literary output.

> To follow Mr. Poe's own apparently frank mode of reviewing, I will begin by putting the merits of my author 'in the fairest light.' I shall not pretend to deny then that he has written several pieces of very considerable merit, and that some of these pieces have attracted, partly of their own accord and partly through the puffing of his friends, an unusual degree of notoriety. Among these I feel called upon to mention his Tales published by Wiley & Putnam, and especially the one called 'The Murders in the Rue Morgue,' which I learn has been reprinted and highly complimented in Paris, and 'The Gold Bug' which Martin Farquhar Tupper justly praises, as well as the 'Descent into the Maelstrom,' and several other stories, all of which I am willing to admit display great power of analysis and imagination.... Some of his shorter poems are also praiseworthy, and his

'Sleeper' and 'Dreamland' are in my opinion better than the Raven, although in a different way.

After Poe, the dime novel supplied plenty of excitement for the youth of the country. These publications should not be neglected by the historian of fiction, even though they were held in great contempt in the petticoat era of the eighteen-eighties. How many men today, I wonder, can look back in memory to see a little boy in a haymow, reading surreptitiously the exploits of Deadwood Dick and others? This was also the lurid era of Gaboriau and his confrères.

Robert Louis Stevenson must have a prominent place in the gallery of great mystery writers. 'The Body Snatcher,' written in June, 1881, and 'Markheim,' which appeared in *Unwin's Annual* of 1886, are fascinating stories. But Stevenson's fame in this connection will always rest upon 'The Strange Case of Doctor Jekyll and Mr. Hyde.' In the Pierpont Morgan Library in New York there is a manuscript of this world-famous story, and I have the first autograph draft. Mrs. Stevenson always believed that this first draft had been entirely destroyed. She was mistaken. Graham Balfour, in his 'Life of Stevenson,' gives, on the authority of Lloyd Osbourne, an interesting but inaccurate account of the genesis of this famous story, and the fate of the first draft:

> A subject much in his [Stevenson's] thought at this time [March, 1885] was the duality of man's nature and the alternation of good and evil; and he was for a long time casting about for a story to embody this central idea. Out of this frame of mind had

scepticism; I shall die, but I shall die incredulous. As for the moral turpitude that man unveiled to me, it is matter that I disdain to handle. He found me an elderly, a useful and a happy man; that he has blighted and sentenced what remains to me of life, is but a small addendum to the monstrous tale of his misdeeds   Hastie Lanyon.

Henry Jekyll's Full Statement of the Case

I was born in the year 1830 to a good fortune, endued with good parts, inclined by nature to industry, fond of the respect of the wise and good among my fellow men, and thus, as it might have been supposed, with every guarantee of an honourable and distinguished future. From a very early age, however, I became in secret the slave of disgraceful pleasures; and when I reached years of reflection, and began to look round me and to take...

MANUSCRIPT OF THE 'STRANGE CASE OF DOCTOR JEKYLL AND MR. HYDE'

come the sombre imagination of Markheim, but that
was not what he required. The true story still de-
layed, till suddenly one night he had a dream. He
awoke and found himself in possession of two, or
rather three, of the scenes in the Strange Case of
Doctor Jekyll and Mr. Hyde. . . . He dreamed these
scenes in considerable detail, including the circum-
stance of the transforming powders, and so vivid was
the impression that he wrote the story off in a red
heat, just as it had been presented to him in his
sleep. . . .

Mrs. Stevenson, according to the custom of the
time, wrote her detailed criticism of the story. . . .
She gave the paper to her husband and left the room.
After a while his bell rang; on her return she found
him sitting up in bed, the clinical thermometer in his
mouth, pointing with a long denunciatory finger to a
pile of ashes. He had burned the entire draft . . . not
out of pique, but from a fear that he might be tempted
to make too much use of it and not rewrite the whole
from a new standpoint.

One afternoon last year I walked through the
underground receiving rooms of a great English firm
of auctioneers in London, with Mr. Rham, a friend
long connected with the firm. The eighteenth-century building on New Bond Street stands upon a
foundation interlaced with arches, somewhat like the
ancient catacombs.

'What a place for a murder!' I remarked, peering
into the dark recesses.

'Sorry, Doctor,' Rham replied, 'but I'm afraid
nothing exciting or mysterious ever happened down
here.' Suddenly he stopped. 'That's odd — apropos

of your remark. Do you see those boxes there?'
Several large packing-cases blocked an archway.
'They contain Conan Doyle's crime library. Every
volume he used for reference when he created Sherlock Holmes and his countless adventures! We are
selling them next month.'

Almost before the words were out of Rham's
mouth, I grasped his arm.

'I must have those books!' I said.

Strange and unexpected are the vagaries of the
book business. I had imagined I should have a hard
fight, financially and perhaps otherwise, to remove
those treasures from England. I had to leave London
before the sale took place, but I left a large, elastic
bid on the Conan Doyle library. Surprised and delighted, several weeks later, I learned by cable in
New York that these volumes were now mine, and all
for ninety-five pounds!

When the collection arrived, I had it placed in my
private book room and opened immediately. All that
night I read.

Noted trials and intricate detailed court records;
stories of famous crimes and great criminals. This
assemblage included two of the most famous collections of crime books — the Newgate Calendar and
the New Newgate Calendar. Then there was Bor-
row's 'Celebrated Trials,' six volumes, 1825. These
two collections have supplied more plots for recent
mystery novels than any other, and there's enough
material in them, untouched, for a hundred new
ones.

Often I paused, wondering which volume in the collection was the inspiration that created Sir Arthur's noted hero. I don't mind admitting that I felt an extraordinary emotion when I saw his signature on the flyleaf of each volume, sometimes alone, sometimes with the autograph of Sir W. S. Gilbert, who had once owned a part of the collection. My pulse quickened, too, as I came across marginal comments and notes by Doyle, indicating the trend of the author's mind at the time.

In London in 1887, a Christmas annual — *Beeton's* — was issued, which was to revolutionize detective fiction. The modest entrance of Sherlock Holmes and his friendly foil, Doctor Watson, occurred in this annual. In a story entitled 'A Study in Scarlet,' C. Auguste Dupin and Monsieur Lecoq met a rival worthy of their mettle. Here was the true scientific investigator, the clever competitor of the C. I. D. of Scotland Yard. Almost in the flesh appeared this really great detective, drawn with such remarkable skill that he attracted the public at once. Now the mystery story was given a new life, while the public was amused by Holmes's comments upon the different brands of pipe tobacco, and how they could be identified. Even the ashes received due consideration, as amateur detectives sprang up everywhere.

Poe received one hundred dollars for 'The Gold-Bug,' but Conan Doyle received only three guineas for his first story. I have many of the Sherlock Holmes manuscripts. 'The Return of Sherlock Holmes,' which was awaited so breathlessly by readers all over the world, is written in three ordinary ruled copy-books, such as school-children in the first grades use! On the covers, under a design of daisies and the name, 'Paragon Exercise Book,' is Doyle's signature and address, Undershaw, Hindhead. The lines are almost without correction, so smoothly did the story flow.

Fergus Hume, who died not long ago, issued his great story, 'The Mystery of a Hansom Cab,' at the same time as the appearance of 'A Study in Scarlet.' This story of Hume's was also received with an acclaim accorded to few detective stories. Its success was instantaneous and, I understand, brought the publishers, but not the writer — as so often happens — a sizable fortune.

I regret I have not the space to devote to Anna Katherine Green and her really great story, 'The Leavenworth Case,' or to the creations of G. K. Chesterton, Edgar Wallace, Agatha Christie, H. C. Bailey, Carolyn Wells, Dorothy L. Sayers, M. P. Shiel, Mary Roberts Rinehart, E. Phillips Oppenheim, E. W. Hornung, Dashiell Hammett, J. S. Fletcher, S. S. Van Dine, Melville Davisson Post, Earl Derr Biggers, Erle Stanley Gardner, and a score of others. Some of the stories running today in the detective magazines are as fine as those of some of the 'classical' writers. I would sooner miss my breakfast than one of these magazines.

I think the five greatest detectives in the world of fiction are, in order:

C. Auguste Dupin
Sherlock Holmes
Monsieur Lecoq
Father Brown
Sergeant Cuff

Of course, no one will agree with me!

It is a pity that some of the places where celebrated murders of the past have been committed haven't been properly marked. That house in Rugeley, England, for instance, where William Palmer poisoned his many victims, is visited by hundreds of morbid pilgrims each year. An interesting story is told of an incident that once took place. A gentleman visiting Palmer's old home at Rugeley was one day approached by a gentle-looking little old lady, who stopped him and stated very proudly that she was the mother of William Palmer!

Letters of famous murderers are interesting. It is not the fate of collectors to obtain such interesting relics, which one sees in the Black Museum of New Scotland Yard. These ghastly trinkets are the property of the English nation, and rightly so. I remember when I was first shown through this famous collection by Sir Trevor Bigham I was shocked — although I have been called a pirate myself! — by the display of plaster casts of the heads of famous criminals with the marks of the rope plainly seen on their necks! How I envied their possession of the little lantern by which one of the most famous murderers was identified and later hanged, and which remains one

of the glories — I should say gories — of Scotland
Yard. I have to be satisfied with autograph letters of
notorious criminals, from Robert Catesby to Landru
and Doctor Crippen. I cannot refrain from quoting
the following ingenious letter from Guiteau, the
slayer of President Garfield:

Strictly Private

Mr. Reed: I will give you and Mr. Merrick & Gen.
Butler & Judge Magruder my note payable one year
hence, for $5000 each if you get me out of here. I
think you can do it on the ground of the nonjurisdic-
tion of the court. I have just written to my brother to
make this offer to Gen. Butler and Judge Magruder.
I depend on him to secure these gentlemen, and I depend on you to secure Mr. Merrick. Please call with
Mr. Merrick without delay. I believe I could make
$50000 next winter lecturing if I get out of this. I
have an offer of $500 per night, for six months from
Boston now.

Yours truly

CHARLES GUITEAU

U. S. Jail,
Washington, D.C.
Feb. 11, 82.

I myself have been the 'victim' of a tale. In an
amusing mystery story, 'The Yorkshire Moorland
Murder,' published a year or two ago, the author,
Mr. J. S. Fletcher, thinly and flatteringly veils my
identity under the name Doctor Charles Essenheim.

Early in the story, I am discovered dead in a wild
bit of country on a Yorkshire moor! It seems that I
had spent the night before — as meritoriously as any
movie star — alone with my books at a little inn, The

Washington, Saturday Evening
June 18 — 1881.

I intended to remove the President
this morning at the depot as he took
the cars for Long Branch; but Mrs
Garfield looked so thin and clung
so tenderly to the President's arm, my
heart failed me to part them, and I
decided to take him alone It will be
no worse for Mrs Garfield; dear soul, to
part with her husband this way, than by
natural death. He is liable to go at
any time; any way,

C. G.

This is the original of the memorable letter written by
Charles Guiteau just two weeks before he
shot President Garfield and probably had as
much to do with hanging the assassin,
as any evidence produced during the trial,
as it showed clearly, the premeditation of
the crime.   C. A. B

LETTER OF CHARLES GUITEAU, TWO WEEKS BEFORE
HE SHOT PRESIDENT GARFIELD

Mr Reed

I will give you & Mr Merrick &
Gen Butler & Judge Magruder my
note payable one year hence, for
$5.000. each, if you get me out of
here. I think you can do it on the
ground. of the non jurisdiction
of the Court. I have just written to
my brother to make this offer to Gen
Butler & Judge Magruder. I depend
on him to secure these gentlemen and I
depend on you to secure Mr Merrick
Please call with Mr Merrick without
delay.

LETTER OF CHARLES GUITEAU, AFTER THE ASSASSINATION
OF PRESIDENT GARFIELD

149

I presume I could make $5000 next winter lecturing if I get out of this.

I have an offer of $75 or $50 per night, for six nights from Boston now.

Yours truly

Charles Guiteau

U.S. Jail
Washington D.C.
Feb 11-82

Muzzled Ox. When a shepherd boy found me, stiff and stark at a lonely spot, Harlesdon Scar, I had one small volume tucked into the pocket of my 'lounge suit,' a first edition of Bunyan's 'Pilgrim's Progress.'

It is strange that just before this story appeared, I had been at York, 'despoiling,' as the English papers later put it, the great library of York Minster. If, however, I am found dead with a book in my pocket, I hope it will be, not 'The Pilgrim's Progress,' but the first edition of 'The Murders in the Rue Morgue'!

IV

EXTRA! EXTRA!

'BLOODY butchery by the British Troops!' As I looked again at the large sheet of paper before me, with its heavy black type, I asked myself if I wasn't reading a *modern* extra. No! It was the first news of the battle of Concord, in its original form, as it had been excitedly pasted upon buildings and fences, and nailed to the peaceful New England elms. Thus it was issued, not unlike our contemporary theatrical posters, exactly one hundred and sixty-one years ago, so that all who ran might read. In those primitive days, long before the telegraph was invented, this was the only way news could be rapidly spread over the countryside. Runners and men on horseback were dispatched from the various villages and settlements where the news had originated. Post-haste they rushed to the nearest printing office, and in a short time the inhabitants beheld the startling headlines. They were the forerunners of the extra of today, and display type was placed at the top of the broadsheet.

In the case of the battle of Concord, in addition to the bloody butchery announcement, a short, gripping tale was told of the runaway fight of the regular troops of His Britannic Majesty against a few hundred provincials, natives of the Massachusetts Bay Colony, who fought it out on April 19, 1775. Of all the grim details given, I think the following paragraph concerns us most:

> These particulars are now published in this cheap form, at the request of the friends of the deceased WORTHIES, who died gloriously fighting in the cause of liberty and their country, and it is their sincere desire that every Householder in the country, who are sincere well-wishers to America, may be possessed of the same, either to frame and glass, or otherwise to preserve in their houses, not only as a token of Gratitude to the memory of the Deceased Forty Persons, but as a perpetual memorial of that important event, on which, perhaps, may depend the future Freedom and Greatness of the Commonwealth of America.

There were thousands of 'well-wishers to America' who received this broadside, but only a few copies of the originals were saved. At the same time a black-bordered 'Concord Death List' was issued. I have seen but one copy of this gruesome sheet, with its skull and crossbones decoration. This, the first mortality record of the Revolution, is exceedingly rare in its original state. There is a Biblical rhythm to that list — 'The names of the Provincials who were killed and wounded in the late Engagement with His Majesty's Troops.' Among them you can read such brave old New England names as Caleb Harrington, Jedediah Monroe, Jason Winship, Azael Porter, Jotham Webb, Perley Putnam, and Prince Easterbrooks, 'a negro man.' The clink of flintlock and the hoarse echo of patriotism reverberate through these names.

Other broadsheets of the Massacre of Boston also show pictures of the coffins of the dead patriots, with skulls and crossbones, which make them eternally interesting.

Like school-children scribbling unpleasant remarks about one another on walls, the British soon came out with their own account of the battles of Concord and Lexington in broadside form. It was the quickest way to catch the eye of the people. This broadsheet is also very rare and of utmost historical importance. General Gage's description is 'a circumstantial account of an attack ... on His Majesty's Troops,' ending: 'Thus this unfortunate Affair has happened through the Rashness and Impudence of a few people who began firing on the troops at Lexington.'

A month and a half later, Governor Thomas Gage was trying to mold the colonists' minds with other broadsides. I have an excessively rare one dated June 12, 1775, headed 'A Proclamation,' and printed by a woman, Margaret Draper, in Boston. It is not only said to have been passed around among the inhabitants of Boston, but was also slipped through the lines of the besieging army to uphold their morale as well. It begins, 'Whereas the infatuated multitude who have long suffered themselves to be conducted by certain Well-known incendiaries and traitors,' and ends with an offer, in His Majesty's name, of 'His most gracious pardon to all rebels, with the exception

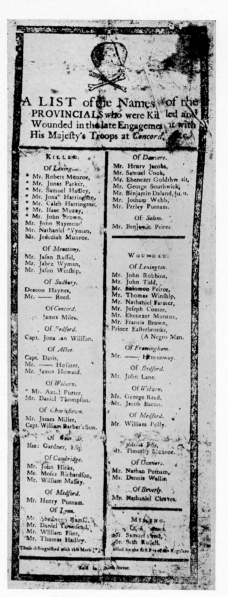

CONCORD DEATH LIST

of Samuel Adams and John Hancock, if they will lay down their arms.'

This broadside is printed in such tiny type as to make it almost unreadable. I doubt if it made much impression. Bolder effects in those days were necessary.

Broadsheets were the first stop-press bulletins, though I prefer the homely extra of our own news-boys. The entire history of America can be written from them, because they may be studied from the year 1639, when the first printing shop was established in this country.

We can trace graphically, step by step, almost every important event in our history, long before we issued newspapers, through these sheets, which were circulated quickly, to give the settlers local news and the important events as reported by recently arrived sailing ships from overseas. In the latter case the news was generally more than five weeks late, but that made little difference to the Puritans, who had but few leisure moments, on account of having to protect their homes from the Indians and the machinations of the French. I think they were just as happy as we are today, receiving their news several weeks late. The greatest news item in the world's history — the Discovery of America by Columbus — was about seven months in reaching Spain.

The Freeman's Oath is the earliest and one of the most important of all American broadsides. Stephen Daye, of Cambridge, Massachusetts, issued it in 1639. It is odd that although the original draft, in the auto-

graph of Governor John Winthrop, has been saved —
it is now one of the prized possessions of the Boston
Public Library — none of the first printed copies has
ever turned up. The earliest contemporary reprints
of the Oath are dated 1647. Every man who was
more than twenty and had been six months a house-
holder was obliged to take the Freeman's Oath before
he could become a fullfledged citizen of the Massachusetts Bay Colony.

It would not surprise me to hear some day that a
copy of the Freeman's Oath had been discovered,
after all these years, waiting to be found beneath the
rafters of one of the old New England farmhouses.
Or perhaps someone has a copy and gives it little consideration because of certain notions concerning the
methods used by Massachusetts' early rulers. I do
hope such an unsuspecting person will come my
way!

This reminds me of the time I visited an old house
near Philadelphia several years ago. It was built in
the time of the first proprietor of Pennsylvania,
William Penn. The family who lived there were of
Quaker origin, but later became staunch members of
the Episcopal Church. As my host and I walked about
the place he surprised me with a bitter tirade about his
Quaker antecedents. When his venom had run its
course, I asked him why he felt as he did, and he
replied he had but little use for the Quakers, because
they had had a too restraining influence in Philadelphia in the early days, and their conservative policies
had, in his opinion, retarded the city's progress.

AT THE TOWN-HOUSE in

BOSTON:

April 18th. 1689

SIR,

OUr Selves as well as many others the Inhabitants of this Town and Places adjacent, being surprized with the Peoples sudden taking to Arms, in the first motion whereof we were wholly ignorant, are driven by the present Exigence and Necessity to acquaint your *Excellency*, that for the Quieting and Security of the People Inhabiting this Countrey from the imminent Dangers they many wayes lie open, and are exposed unto, and for your own Safety; We judge it necessary that you forthwith Surrender, and Deliver up the Government and Fortifications to be Preserved, to be Disposed according to Order and Direction from the Crown of *England*, which is suddenly expected may Arrive, Promising all Security from violence to your Self, or any other of your Gentlemen and Souldiers in Person or Estate: or else we are assured they will endeavour the taking of the Fortifications by Storm, if any opposition be made.

To *Sr. Edmond Andross Knight.*

William Stoughton.	*Simon Bradstreet.*	*Wait Winthrop.*
Thomas Danforth.	*John Richards.*	*Samuel Shrimpton.*
	Elisha Cook.	*William Brown.*
	Isaac Addington,	*Barthol. Gidney.*
	John Foster·	
	Peter Sergeant.	
	David Waterhouse.	
	Adam Winthrop.	
	John Nelson.	

Boston Printed by *Samuel Green.* 1639.

BROADSIDE CALL TO SIR EDMOND ANDROSS TO SURRENDER
BOSTON

'I've only one thing left of all my Quaker belongings,' he said, 'and I don't know why I've kept that! It's a confounded old sheet of paper concerning a Quaker meeting in Burlington.'

'What's the date?' I inquired casually.

'1692,' he replied. 'Would you like to see it?'

Presently I spread a yellowed roll of paper on the table before me. Imagine my delight when I read William Bradford's name in the corner — the first printer in the Middle Colonies! This broadside was unknown to me and I believed it to be unique. The owner was anxious to dispose of it at any price — even a low one — all because of his dislike of Quakers. Incidentally, a particularly rich one had died and failed to mention him in his will! And now for the dénouement. I took the broadside to New York. It was perfect except for one corner which had been torn off some time during the past two hundred years. One day when Doctor Wilberforce Eames and I sat in my library discussing the eternal subject of Americana, I showed him my latest find. In his quiet manner he studied it silently for a moment. Finally he said he believed he could complete it — supply the missing corner. Such a rash statement from so conservative a gentleman amused me. I smiled unbelievingly. A day or so later he came from his office in the New York Public Library and brought a little parcel with him. He opened it and shook out several torn pieces of yellowed paper onto the library table. Then he selected a triangular segment with a ragged edge and held it to the torn corner of my broadside. It fitted perfectly, and I actually felt as though I were beholding magic or some miracle of Saint Francis.

Once upon a time I came into possession of William Penn's own copy of the original map of Pennsylvania used by him in his celebrated lawsuit with Lord Baltimore, concerning the boundary line — drawn in Penn's own hand — between Pennsylvania and Maryland. It seemed to me that its final resting-place should be in the library at the State Capitol. With this in mind I journeyed to Harrisburg. I had already told my idea to a political friend and he forthwith introduced a bill for its purchase. It was my first and I may say my only experience in lobbying. The bill was passed, but to tell the truth it was hard work to enthuse a lot of unimaginative state senators over this project of mine. After a great deal of persuasion it was accomplished. Then there was a final step — that of persuading the governor to sign the bill. When I found that my new rôle as a lobbyist had been — as I thought — successful, I began to wander about the Harrisburg streets, instinctively taking the direction of the second-hand bookshops. In one the proprietor showed me a small broadside advertising real estate for sale in Pennsylvania in 1786. This, a tract of land in Centre County, was previously settled by an ancestor of mine, Aaron Levy. His broadside was a public announcement by him to sell the land in parcels so that he might with characteristic modesty name the town — which he did — after himself, Aaronsburg.

BOOK ROOM IN PHILADELPHIA

I had already heard of this broadside; in fact, had been searching for it for many years. For sentimental reasons I felt I must have it. Perhaps I showed undue interest when the dealer placed it in my hands, for he asked me the ridiculously high price of five hundred dollars. Although it was worth that to me, it couldn't possibly have been worth so much to anyone else. I remonstrated with him, but he quickly shut me up with, 'Why, Doctor Rosenbach offered me four hundred and twenty-five dollars for it!' Although this was a lie out of whole cloth, I replied firmly, 'I cannot offer more than Doctor Rosenbach!' and secured it for the lower figure.

My ancestors were poor business men. Lots sixty feet by two hundred were offered for six dollars each! I could have bought seventy lots in the old town for the price of this broadside.

In the midst of a summer shower one afternoon several years ago, a friend rushed into my office dripping rain as he clutched to his breast a brown paper parcel. He was apparently very much excited, but unfastened the string as carefully as though he were handling a newborn babe. 'Alas,' I sighed to myself, 'will people never learn that merely because something has existed for a hundred years or so, that does not mean it has value?' I noted the wild glint of triumph in his eye — that glint which indicates the intense suffering of the amateur discoverer of rarities. On the desk before me he scattered a great assortment of old newspapers and broadsheets. He muttered to himself and I learned that he had spent the last two hours chasing a dump cart on its way to the paper mill.

He was so completely enamored of what he called his 'find' that I did not have the heart to let him see my reaction. And although sorely tempted, as he flashed one sheet after another before my face, I kept my manners and did not inform him that thousands of similar bundles containing old newspapers, broadsheets, and handbills were brought and sent to me every year by just such excited dolts as he. Further, that from such hodgepodge sources I seldom found anything of the slightest interest.

Yet that day had not been an entirely unhappy one for me. A generous and unusually human collector had presented me with an amusing broadside, an undated but authentic Revolutionary sheet with the original verses of 'Yankee Doodle' printed upon it, and embellished with quaint woodcuts purporting to be life likenesses of Washington's soldiers. Therefore I felt in the best of humor. So, to pacify my temporarily demented friend, I promised to examine his collection immediately, that very afternoon. He went away in a high state of exultation and I began my work. I had almost reached the bottom of the pile when a sudden gust of wind and rain blew up Walnut Street and into my very window, and neatly lifted every paper, this way and that, to the floor. I leaned down to gather together this precious assortment when I stopped suddenly in my tracks, my eyes glued to the carpet. Staring at me from one corner were the words, 'Boston, November 20, 1772.' I picked up

this broadside quickly and read an impassioned appeal to the people of the colonies to free themselves
from British tyranny. It begins as follows:

> Gentlemen: We, the Freeholders and other Inhabit-
> ants of Boston, in Town-Meeting duly assembled,
> according to Law, apprehending this is abundant
> Reason to be alarmed that the Plan of Despotism,
> which the Enemies of our invaluable Rights have
> concerted, is rapidly hastening to a completion, can
> no longer conceal our impatience under a constant,
> unremitted, uniform Aid to inslave us, or confide in
> an Administration which threatens us with certain
> and inevitable destruction. . . .

I recognized it as a scarce, indeed an excessively
rare broadside, known among collectors as the very
first to incite directly and publicly the impulse for
united action and revolution within colonial breasts.
Here was drama indeed — this broadside of utmost
historical importance. There are very few copies of it
today, although thousands were circulated at the time
to every hill and vale of the colonies. William Cooper,
the town clerk of Boston, had affixed his signature to
it with bold and determined strokes. I have often
wondered if any of Cooper's descendants were wise
enough to save this or any of the several important
broadsides bearing his name. How thrilling they are!
You can feel and almost see the colonists' fury rise
and expand with each new proclamation!

In this you may learn one of the secrets of the lure
of broadsides. They are the sirens who beckon
aged-in-the-wood bookmen off the beaten track of

book-collecting. I would put aside the most exciting detective story ever written to read any Revolutionary sheet, for though mere scraps of paper they
are filled with magic which interprets the era in sharp,
broad lines that the years can never soften. Yes, they
are the real pulse of the day and throb with the news
of the moment. As most of these moments happened
to be martial and revolutionary, the broadside must
thrill every collector of Americana who has a drop of
patriotic blood running through his veins.

In honor of the Sesquicentennial Exhibition we
showed many Revolutionary relics in the windows of
our Philadelphia store. One day a woman stood outside for a long time looking at these things; then suddenly came in and insisted upon seeing me. She
said she had an ancient broadside that had been in her
family ever since it was issued. When I asked her its
contents and the date, she replied it was a broadside
of the Declaration of Independence, issued in Philadelphia, July 4, 1776.

As there are but three or four copies known to
exist of the Philadelphia issue, I was naturally skep-
tical. But she stuck to her story and said she was a
direct descendant of one of the Signers. I had heard
such stories before.

I told her to bring me the broadside the following
day. I had forgotten until the next morning that it
was a national holiday, July Fourth. Nevertheless, I
kept the appointment and was really well repaid, because the broadside proved to be the genuine article.
To me it was a particularly fitting celebration to be-

A DECLARATION

By the REPRESENTATIVES of the

UNITED STATES OF AMERICA,

In GENERAL CONGRESS ASSEMBLED.

WHEN in the Course of human Events, it becomes necessary for one People to dissolve the Political Bands which have connected them with another, and to assume among the Powers of the Earth, the separate and equal Station to which the Laws of Nature and of Nature's God entitle them, a decent Respect to the Opinions of Mankind requires that they should declare the causes which impel them to the Separation.

We hold these Truths to be self-evident, that all Men are created equal, that they are endowed by their Creator with certain unalienable Rights, that among these are Life, Liberty, and the Pursuit of Happiness—That to secure these Rights, Governments are instituted among Men, deriving their just Powers from the Consent of the Governed, that whenever any Form of Government becomes destructive of these Ends, it is the Right of the People to alter or to abolish it, and to institute new Government, laying its Foundation on such Principles, and organizing its Powers in such Form, as to them shall seem most likely to effect their Safety and Happiness. Prudence, indeed, will dictate that Governments long established should not be changed for light and transient Causes; and accordingly all Experience hath shewn, that Mankind are more disposed to suffer, while Evils are sufferable, than to right themselves by abolishing the Forms to which they are accustomed. But when a long Train of Abuses and Usurpations, pursuing invariably the same Object, evinces a Design to reduce them under absolute Despotism, it is their Right, it is their Duty, to throw off such Government, and to provide new Guards for their future Security. Such has been the patient Sufferance of these Colonies; and such is now the Necessity which constrains them to alter their former Systems of Government. The History of the present King of Great-Britain is a History of repeated Injuries and Usurpations, all having in direct Object the Establishment of an absolute Tyranny over these States. To prove this, let Facts be submitted to a candid World.

He has refused his Assent to Laws, the most wholesome and necessary for the public Good.

He has forbidden his Governors to pass Laws of immediate and pressing Importance, unless suspended in their Operation till his Assent should be obtained; and when so suspended, he has utterly neglected to attend to them.

He has refused to pass other Laws for the Accommodation of large Districts of People, unless those People would relinquish the Right of Representation in the Legislature, a Right inestimable to them, and formidable to Tyrants only.

He has called together Legislative Bodies at Places unusual, uncomfortable, and distant from the Depository of their public Records, for the sole Purpose of fatiguing them into Compliance with his Measures.

He has dissolved Representative Houses repeatedly, for opposing with manly Firmness his Invasions on the Rights of the People.

He has refused for a long Time, after such Dissolutions, to cause others to be elected; whereby the Legislative Powers, incapable of Annihilation, have returned to the People at large for their exercise; the State remaining in the mean time exposed to all the Dangers of Invasion from without, and Convulsions within.

He has endeavoured to prevent the Population of these States; for that Purpose obstructing the Laws for Naturalization of Foreigners; refusing to pass others to encourage their Migrations hither, and raising the Conditions of new Appropriations of Lands.

He has obstructed the Administration of Justice, by refusing his Assent to Laws for establishing Judiciary Powers.

He has made Judges dependent on his Will alone, for the Tenure of their Offices, and the Amount and Payment of their Salaries.

He has erected a Multitude of new Offices, and sent hither Swarms of Officers to harass our People, and eat out their Substance.

He has kept among us, in Times of Peace, Standing Armies, without the consent of our Legislatures.

He has affected to render the Military independent of and superior to the Civil Power.

He has combined with others to subject us to a Jurisdiction foreign to our Constitution, and unacknowledged by our Laws; giving his Assent to their Acts of pretended Legislation:

For quartering large Bodies of Armed Troops among us:

For protecting them, by a mock Trial, from Punishment for any Murders which they should commit on the Inhabitants of these States:

For cutting off our Trade with all Parts of the World:

For imposing Taxes on us without our Consent:

For depriving us, in many Cases, of the Benefits of Trial by Jury:

For transporting us beyond Seas to be tried for pretended Offences:

For abolishing the free System of English Laws in a neighbouring Province, establishing therein an arbitrary Government, and enlarging its Boundaries, so as to render it at once an Example and fit Instrument for introducing the same absolute Rule into these Colonies:

For taking away our Charters, abolishing our most valuable Laws, and altering fundamentally the Forms of our Governments:

For suspending our own Legislatures, and declaring themselves invested with Power to legislate for us in all Cases whatsoever.

He has abdicated Government here, by declaring us out of his Protection and waging War against us.

He has plundered our Seas, ravaged our Coasts, burnt our Towns, and destroyed the Lives of our People.

He is, at this Time, transporting large Armies of foreign Mercenaries to compleat the Works of Death, Desolation and Tyranny, already begun with circumstances of Cruelty and Perfidy, scarcely paralleled in the most barbarous Ages, and totally unworthy the Head of a civilized Nation.

He has constrained our fellow Citizens taken Captive on the high Seas to bear Arms against their Country, to become the Executioners of their Friends and Brethren, or to fall themselves by their Hands.

He has excited domestic Insurrections amongst us, and has endeavoured to bring on the Inhabitants of our Frontiers, the merciless Indian Savages, whose known Rule of Warfare, is an undistinguished Destruction, of all Ages, Sexes and Conditions.

In every stage of these Oppressions we have Petitioned for Redress in the most humble Terms: Our repeated Petitions have been answered only by repeated Injury. A Prince, whose Character is thus marked by every act which may define a Tyrant, is unfit to be the Ruler of a free People.

Nor have we been wanting in Attentions to our British Brethren. We have warned them from Time to Time of Attempts by their Legislature to extend an unwarrantable Jurisdiction over us. We have reminded them of the Circumstances of our Emigration and Settlement here. We have appealed to their native Justice and Magnanimity, and we have conjured them by the Ties of our common Kindred to disavow these Usurpations, which, would inevitably interrupt our Connections and Correspondence. They too have been deaf to the Voice of Justice and of Consanguinity. We must, therefore, acquiesce in the Necessity, which denounces our Separation, and hold them, as we hold the rest of Mankind, Enemies in War, in Peace, Friends.

We, therefore, the Representatives of the UNITED STATES OF AMERICA, in GENERAL CONGRESS, Assembled, appealing to the Supreme Judge of the World for the Rectitude of our Intentions, do, in the Name, and by Authority of the good People of these Colonies, solemnly Publish and Declare, That these United Colonies are, and of Right ought to be, FREE AND INDEPENDENT STATES; that they are absolved from all Allegiance to the British Crown, and that all political Connection between them and the State of Great-Britain, is and ought to be totally dissolved; and that as FREE AND INDEPENDENT STATES, they have full Power to levy War, conclude Peace, contract Alliances, establish Commerce, and to do all other Acts and Things which INDEPENDENT STATES may of right do. And for the support of this Declaration, with a firm Reliance on the Protection of divine Providence, we mutually pledge to each other our Lives, our Fortunes, and our sacred Honor.

Signed by Order and in Behalf of the Congress,

JOHN HANCOCK, President.

Attest.
CHARLES THOMSON, Secretary.

Philadelphia: Printed by John Dunlap.

DECLARATION OF INDEPENDENCE, PHILADELPHIA, JOHN DUNLAP

come its owner exactly one hundred and fifty years, to the day, after its issue.

To my mind, the Declaration broadside is one of the most interesting and valuable in the whole range of Americana. It certainly makes the pulse beat quicker when we read, 'When in the Course of human events ——'

To read it from a school-book or in a dry-as-dust historical primer is one thing; to read it in its original form as printed by John Dunlap in Philadelphia is quite another.

It brings back, as one glances at the time-stained paper, the very sheet that gave the inhabitants the first news of its adoption, a vision of those times unequaled in any history.

This broadside was issued, not only in the city of the signing, but in New York, Baltimore, Salem, Massachusetts, and in other towns. They are all valuable. One I have, printed in Salem, is particularly interesting. On the back is written:

> Independence declared July 4th 1776 Rec.d and read to my people August 18th
>
> I Backus.

During the period that pleas were being issued against the Colonies by groups of loyalists and adherents of the British Government, private individuals and general officers as well posted their opinions in the same way. I have one of three copies known of a proclamation issued by Benedict Arnold. In it he loosened the rancor and spite he had nursed for years, and displayed his religious intolerance and his desire to inflame patriotism on that unfair ground.

To my mind, the broadsides issued by the loyalists and those in sympathy with Great Britain are just as important to the historian of the Revolution as those printed by the seceding colonists. There is no doubt that the early American accounts are too highly colored, to put it pleasantly. The patriots were too near the scene to write dispassionately. George III was painted as a terrible ogre, with a face to frighten little children, instead of an amiable old gentleman attending to his kingly duties.

Broadsides are not so easily discovered as books. You can't search with such avidity for sheets of paper as you can for more substantial items. It seems only natural for a collector to rummage through strange places for books. They and pamphlets — anything in book form — are easier to handle than large sheets of paper.

Once when motoring through some woodland near Easton, Maryland, a hilly country of scattered farmhouses, I stopped on the outskirts of a small town to inquire my way.

I did not realize, as I drew up before a tumbledown shack, that it was a restaurant of sorts, a lunch-wagon made from a defunct freight car — a choice bit of Americana in itself.

As I stood in the open doorway to inquire of the proprietor, an elderly man, I was rendered almost speechless as I saw a sheet of printed paper tacked on the wall behind him.

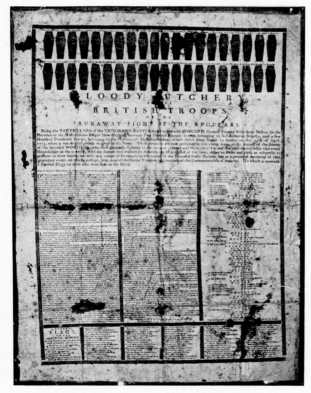

Monday Morning, December 27, 1773.

THE Tea-Ship being arrived, every Inhabitant who wishes to preserve the Liberty of America, is desired to meet at the STATE-HOUSE, This Morning, precisely at TEN o'Clock, to advise what is best to be done on this alarming Crisis.

TEA SHIP BROADSIDE

BLOODY BUTCHERY OF THE BRITISH TROOPS

To make a long story short, I not only got the directions I sought, but for a very modest sum the broadside that caught my eye. And where it came from the owner said that he did not know. It was a piece of trash he had found in a bundle of newspapers and tacked over a knot-hole in the wood. It was the famous Tea pronouncement.

> At a meeting of the People of Boston and the neighboring Towns at Faneuil Hall, in said Boston on Monday the 29th of November 1773, nine o'clock and continued by adjournment to the next day for the Purpose of consulting, advising and Determining upon the most proper and effectual method to prevent the unloading receiving or vending the detestable Tea sent out by the East-India Company, part of which being just arrived in the Harbour.

Then there is the even more stirring Philadelphia Tea Ship broadside, issued two days earlier:

> To the Delaware Pilots. Now we took the Pleasure, some Days since, of kindly admonishing you to do your Duty; if perchance you should meet with the (Tea) Ship Polly, Captain Ayres; a Three Decker which is hourly expected. . . . There is some Talk of a Handsome Reward for the Pilot who gives the first good Account of her. . . . But all agree, that Tar and Feathers will be his Portion, who pilots her into this Harbour.
>
> THE COMMITTEE FOR TARRING AND FEATHERING.

This broadside was the second of two expressly written to warn the Delaware pilots.

There is also a letter on the same sheet addressed to the Captain Ayres mentioned in the warning, in which the excited Philadelphians tell him:

> In the first Place, we must tell you, that the Pennsylvanians are, to a Man, passionately fond of Freedom; the Birthright of Americans; and at all Events are determined to enjoy it. That they sincerely believe, no Power on the face of the Earth has a Right to tax them without their Consent. That in their Opinion, the Tea in your Custody is designed by the Ministry to enforce such a Tax, which they undoubtedly will oppose.... What think you, Captain, of a Halter around your Neck — ten gallons of liquid Tar decanted on your Pate — with the Feathers of a dozen wild Geese laid over that to enliven your appearance?

Last year a friend came to Philadelphia to check up the estate left him by a great uncle. It was a very pleasant visit, as you can imagine. This uncle had been a lawyer for more than fifty years and his ancient offices on Fourth Street were filled with old legal documents, family letters and papers. It was the ideal place for treasure trove. Mr. Blank spent weeks sorting over barrels and cupboards in the hope, I think, of finding something of importance. At last he unearthed an old newspaper — the *Ulster County Gazette* — dated January 4, 1800. Its edges were printed in deep mourning, and with amazed satisfaction he read the important announcement of the death of General Washington.

You can imagine that my friend wasted little time bringing that newspaper to me. The moment I saw it

I laughed. I had good reason to laugh, too, or to tear my hair! For the ghosts of countless *Ulster County Gazettes* rose up before me. Every year hundreds of people bring me this worthless reprint of an original that exists but in a solitary example.

I explained to Blank that the *Ulster County Gazette* was fast becoming a tiresome joke. Every week some frantic owner, thinking he has found something priceless, sets forth with it to the Public Library in New York. My friend rolled up his copy with some other papers in a very disappointed manner and prepared to leave. But my ears caught a peculiar crackle. Old paper. I detained him.

'What else have you there?'

'Nothing of value. Some verses with no date.'

And he unrolled the bundle to prove it. The verses happened to be a Revolutionary ballad issued on an unusually narrow piece of paper, a very rare broadside. At the top was a woodcut portrait of General Warren, beneath which was printed in large type, 'Americans to Arms.' It was published with similar songs of the same sentiment, such as 'America Triumphant, or Old England's Downfall,' in 1775. This one was sung by our ancestors to the melody 'Britons to Arms!' Here it is:

AMERICANS TO ARMS
(Sung to the Tune of 'Britons to Arms')

America's Sons yourselves prepare,
For Liberty now calls for War,
Exert yourselves with Force and Might,
Show how AMERICANS can fight,

And only to maintain their Right —
Farewell England.

Rouse, rouse, my Boys, 'tis FREEDOM that calls,
Mount, mount your Guns, prepare your Ball;
We'll fight, we'll conquer, or we'll die,
But we'll maintain our LIBERTY,
And hand it to Posterity —
Farewell England.

Hark! from afar, how the Trumpet sounds,
See the bold Heroes in Blood and Wounds;
Drums a beating, Colors flying,
Cannons roaring, brave Men dying,
Such are the bold AMERICANS —
Farewell England.

AMERICA which rules over the Land,
Her valiant Sons join Hand in Hand;
United Sons of FREEDOM may
Drive all those Dogs of War away,
With Triumph crown AMERICA —
Farewell England.

Why then should we be daunted at all,
Since we've engag'd in so noble a Call?
As fighting for our CHURCH and Laws,
And dying in so just a Cause,
'Twill prove the fatal Overthrow — of England.
Quisquis Reipublicae sit infelix, felix esse non potest.
The Cause we fight for animates us high,
Namely RELIGION and dear LIBERTY.

One of the most famous of all Revolutionary
ballads is Francis Hopkinson's 'The Battle of the
Kegs.' Although it first appeared on March 4, 1778,
in the *Pennsylvania Packet,* its popularity grew until

it was set to music and sung by the soldiers at the front. Later it appeared as a pamphlet and then as a broadside. The author was so pleased at its unexpected popularity that he sent a special copy in his autograph to Benjamin Franklin.

On December 17, 1777, the navy board, which was then at Bordentown, sent a letter to Washington containing this mysterious information:

> I have the pleasure of assuring you that everything goes on with Secrecy and Dispatch to the Satisfaction of the Artist. We expect he will be enabled in a day or two to try the important Experiment.

The 'artist' happened to be a talented young inventor, David Bushnell. He produced the first floating mine — he also originated a crude type of submarine — which exploded the moment it came in contact with any foreign object. The first one floated down the Delaware about January 1, 1778. It was barrel-shaped to make it float easily. A story was circulated that these mines were filled with armed rebels who had orders to come forth at dead of night, as the Grecians came from the wooden horse at the siege of Troy. Several imaginative king's soldiers swore they had seen bayonet points sticking through holes in the kegs, and others whispered that the kegs were nothing less than infernal machines constructed by magic, that one could easily destroy a city. In the greatest consternation the British troops opened a fusillade upon every floating object and continued to fire at each keg that floated down the river, including a cask of butter dropped accidentally overboard by an old market woman on her way to town. After all this excitement the British actually dared to announce that they had won a great victory over the colonists. General Howe ordered a fast sailing vessel sent to England to report his splendid triumph.

Hopkinson, who held the British in utmost contempt, was struck by the humor of this victory; he was inspired to write this famous poem, 'The Battle of the Kegs.'

> The motley crew, in vessels new
>   With Satan for their guide, sir,
> Pack'd up in bags or wooden kegs,
>   Came driving down the tide, sir.
>
> A sailor, too, in jerkin blue,
>   This strange appearance viewing,
> First damn'd his eyes in great surprise,
>   Then said, 'Some mischief's brewing.
>
> These Kegs I'm told, the rebels hold,
>   Pack'd up like pickling herring;
> And they've come down t' attack the Town
>   In this new way of ferrying.
>
> Therefore prepare for bloody war,
>   These Kegs must all be routed,
> Or surely we despised shall be,
>   And British courage doubted.'
>
> The cannons roar from shore to shore,
>   The small arms make a rattle;
> Since wars began I'm sure no man
>   E'er saw so strange a battle.

When I first heard our newsboys shout their extras announcing the end of the Great War in 1918, I compared them in my mind's eye with the Revolutionary broadside announcing the Treaty of Peace with Great Britain in 1783. We think our flashing headlines are sensational. What announcement in the late war could have been more breath-taking than the blazing black type of the very rare Cornwallis-surrender broadside? It was much more important to the inhabitants of the colonies than that of the terms of peace which came two years later. It was the last stand of England on this continent and meant that the tired and worn soldiers could return to their homes.

Cornwallis TAKEN!
Boston (Friday) October 26th, 1781. This morning an express arrived from Providence to his Excellency the Governor ... announcing the important Intelligence of the Surrender of Lord Cornwallis and his army....

I have dealt in this article more with war than I intended. Long before the Revolution, before the shots were heard at Concord, the people craved other kinds of excitement. Instead of jazz, airplane accidents, listening to Big Ben strike three thousand miles away, the simple colonists waited for their own extras. They avidly read every scrap of information about the last dying speech of some criminal executed, not in the electric chair but on the more picturesque gallows specially constructed for him. They could hardly wait for the news. Females had a hard time of it, for there was the hateful notice printed in large type at the bottom of the announcement: 'No women or Children will be allowed near the place of execution.' I cannot refrain from giving one of the precious execution broadsides:

For some time past the Public have been anxiously waiting to be informed of the Life, Character and Last Dying words of

JASON FAIRBANKS

But his reservedness at the time of his Execution, and his entire silence to the numerous and most respectful Spectators that were ever known in the United States to assemble on so trying and Melancholy occasion, has disappointed the Public at large with his Speech, which we can only account for but by his possessing an unparalleled share of the depravity of human nature. But we here give a Biography of Mr. JASON FAIRBANKS and MISS ELIZA FALES, containing a sketch of their characters, and relating every incident of moment from their being children to the solemn period of their lives. Also a concise and authentic description of the termination of Miss Fale's Life. The behaviour of Fairbanks at the time of his apprehension. (Written by a Gentleman, residing near Dedham, who has been well acquainted with the parties, and was formerly an inmate at the same School with Fairbanks)

Miss Fales was a model which the pencil of a Raphael might in vain endeavor to delineate! elegance, and symetry in her form were blended. Her luxuriant auburn hair flowed in graceful ringlets round her well turn'd shoulders. Her neck and bosom might with alabaster vie. Her taper waist, her glowing cheeks ting'd with the crimson blush of virgin modesty displayed the most happy assemblage of the carnation

and lily, that ever graced a mortal form. Her graces
collectively considered, presented a living figure of
what our enthusiastic imagination has often portrayed
of the Grecian Helen's.

The Shade of Eliza Fales, assended to the happy regions of paradise.

The mortal part of Eliza Fales is now deposited with
its kindred clay, but that Vital Spark which never
dies, we trust, has been ushered by sister spirits thro'
the etherial regions, into the blissful abodes of Paradise — there to exist with renevated vigor, where life
is one of continued scene of endless extasy — in company with myriads chanting Canto's of Thanksgiving
and Praise to the Deity.

On the top is a picture of a man, hanging, with two
coffins on either side.

Every conceivable article of news appeared on these
early sheets. They were so yellow that the modern
newspaper of this type is a pale *jaune* in comparison
with them. Advertisements for the return of escaped
convicts are particularly appealing. In them the
crimes are minutely described. In 1726 William
Russel, alias Edward Church, a hardened criminal,
could be instantly identified from the following:

Is full fac'd, has dark brown Hair and curl'd, red-
dish Beard, a middling fine Beaver Hat, wears it
flapping, has on a light gray short Jacket, a white
Douless Shirt pretty fine one, Ozenbriggs Frock, But-
tons upon the Shoulders, & close before, a pair of
Wooden-heel Shoes, Nails in the heels.

The notice of the latest burglary was alluringly set
forth, and the colonists awaited the 'freshest advice'

on the important event. Patent medicines and nostrums of every kind, all with miraculous virtues, were advertised. The latest drownings, terrifying tornadoes, sudden deaths, disastrous fires, scandal below and above stairs, were fearfully and minutely described. The old were shocked by them as they are today! Nevertheless, they were read, and how! In 1792, when thirty men, women and children were lost in New York Harbor on a Sunday, the broadside scribbler remarked most righteously that 'they were taking their Pleasure on the Sacred Day.'

When we think of the latest devices for gathering and spreading news — the telegraph, the radio, to say nothing of high-speed presses — we cannot but meditate, with something akin to pity, on the primitive methods of our forefathers.

We should be wrong. If wise old Benjamin Franklin were alive today, hearing of the newest time and labor-saving devices, he would surely exclaim, 'You've saved all this time; now what are you going to do with it?'

V

MIGHTY WOMEN
BOOK HUNTERS

'IS IT possible for a woman to be a bibliophile?'

This is a question that was argued, over a century ago at the breakfast table of the famous collector, Guilbert de Pixérécourt. I can imagine his friends, other collectors and scholars, looking down their long French noses, knitting their brows, and exclaiming, '*C'est impossible, monsieur!*' Would that I might have been present to refute such masculine slander!

Women, someone wittily said, have always been collectors. From the earliest time they have gathered, somewhat mysteriously, the store of the world's luxuries. It was a very modern young lady who aptly voiced the wisdom of her sex, when she said, 'Kissing your hand may make you feel very very good, but a diamond and sapphire bracelet lasts forever.' But in contrast to this, the jewels of the mind have appealed more strongly to some of her wiser sisters.

Today, when women excel in sports, in golf, tennis, swimming, flying, it often amazes me that they do not attempt something equally thrilling and even more adventurous. I suppose that the greatest game of all, the art of love, which women played before the dawn of history, is, and always will be, their own charming province. After love — I say, *after* love — book-collecting is the most exhilarating sport of all.

To glean something of the history of women book-collectors we must travel back five hundred years, to France of the magnificent châteaux, with gay lights o' love, with mistresses of kings, whose naughty flame-colored stockings were once termed blue. What women! They added, not only to the flamboyancy and gaiety of life in the fifteenth and sixteenth centuries, but dared to thumb their pretty noses at Savonarola and Martin Luther, who tried quite unsuccessfully to rob these fair imps of the many pretty ways that so well became them.

Who are they? Their musical names are familiar. Diane de Poitiers, Gabrielle d'Estrées — beloved of Henry IV — Catherine de Medici, Madame de Pompadour, and many others who made French history glittering. While these bewitching creatures dutifully carried exquisitely illuminated breviaries on the Sabbath, and took pride in owning little prayer-books penned by some noted calligrapher, such as Bourdichon or Nicholas Jarry, it was in their boudoirs, in some intimate corner, seductively arranged, that they kept the choicest morsels of Anacreon, of Aristophanes, beautifully bound copies of Ovid, and be-jeweled examples of the 'Heptameron' of the Reine Margot. In those happy days, as you will see, love and book-collecting went hand in hand.

It speaks rather well, I think, for the kings of France that they chose for friends beautiful ladies

DIANE DE POITIERS

MADAME DE VERRUE

who loved beautiful books. What romantic stories must be hidden in these treasures of binding and print. When I behold a royal binding with the interlaced initials of King Henry II and the fair Diane de Poitiers, or come upon a lovely romance of chivalry with the devices of the Great Louis and the crests of Madame de Montespan, I begin at once to ponder on the hidden motive for this regal love of books.

When Henry, second of that name, wooed Diane, did he present to her a jeweled crown, executed by Benvenuto Cellini, or at the height of his infatuation, the Château d'Anet? Your true bibliophile thinks otherwise. He loves to amuse himself with the thought that the most persuasive of the King's gifts was a book. Some glorious volume, with superb illustrations, that would make the frail recipient murmur ecstatically, 'This is *too* much!' The true collector dreams, as he sits in his library, of the golden days when women could be wooed and won by a book! I know several bibliophiles who wish they would soon return!

Women first began to preen themselves as book-collectors in the years immediately preceding the invention of printing. Then the writing of books was such a costly affair that the production was extremely limited. The early libraries consisted almost entirely of hand-written, decorated breviaries, books of hours, missals, lives of the saints, and works by the fathers of the Church. Today these manuscripts are regarded with the greatest affection by the bibliophile, and he considers nothing this side of heaven more

beautiful. The first time he sees the prayer-book of
the Duchesse de Berri, with its magnificent miniatures, or the breviary of the Duchesse de Lorraine, a
feeling of faintness mixed with envy must come over
him. Alas, that such masterpieces are nearly all un-
attainable, locked away in great national libraries.

Louise de Savoie, Duchesse d'Angoulême, twice
regent under her son, Francis I, was one of the first
French women to form an important collection of
books. Born in 1476, just twenty years after the invention of printing, and six years after the first press
was established in Paris, this distinguished mother of
the first Francis did much to encourage the new art
and to make it flourish in France. Among the volumes gathered by Louise de Savoie were the 'Life of
Saint Jerome,' the 'Triumphs of Virtue,' Boccaccio's
'Lives of Noble Ladies,' and a curious work, the
'Epistles of Ovid, or Examples of Letters Suitable
for a Lady to Write to Her Husband.' Among her
possessions was also a lovely manuscript with twenty-
one large miniatures depicting Penelope, Phyllis,
Hermione, and Hero, in costumes of the sixteenth
century. Twenty-five years ago this precious volume
was one of the glories of the Hermitage in St. Peters-
burg. Where is it, I wonder, today?

Another famous bibliophile was the beautiful and
willful Marguerite d'Angoulême, Queen of Navarre,
sister of Francis. Born the year this country was
discovered, she lives forever in the praises of Brantôme, Calvin, and Melanchthon. Rabelais wrote his
greatest eulogy, when he dedicated his immortal

work to 'L'Esprit de la reine de Navarre.' All scholars are conversant with this amazing queen's own literary works, her chansons, poems, her mysteries. Her most renowned work, the 'Heptameron,' did not appear in print until 1558, nine years after her death, although the manuscript was in circulation during her lifetime. These seventy stories were first issued under the title, 'Histoire des Amans Fortunez.' Where is Marguerite's own autograph manuscript of the 'Heptameron'? Many a collector would like to know. Did it ever exist?

The Queen of Navarre had the human qualities necessary to every great collector. To begin with, she was a true daughter of the Renaissance, imaginative, generous. A patroness of poets and of beggars, the companion of courtly ladies and gallant gentlemen, and the delight, too, of precious vagabonds. Booklovers venerate her memory, not only for her charm and erudition, but because of her position among the women bibliophiles of France.

Diane de Poitiers, Duchesse de Valentinois, to whom I have already alluded, was a lady whose pictures reveal a charming mouth, a noble expression, and burning eyes. She became the beloved of Henry II. Born the daughter of a bibliophile, Jean de Poitiers, she was reared from the day of her birth, in 1499, in an atmosphere of scholarship and the sacred traditions of a library. Married at the age of sixteen to Louis de Brézé, grand seneschal of Normandy, her career is the subject of many legendary histories. Ancient chroniclers relate that in order to save her father, who was implicated in the conspiracy of the Constable of Bourbon, she had to sacrifice her honor to Francis I. But bibliophiles have always chosen to disbelieve this somewhat sordid if dramatic story. Considering the literary tastes of both Francis and Diane, we prefer the more reasonable theory that some rare volume was the chief allure. The real problem for the bibliophile is — which one?

In the annals of bibliomania the reign of Henry II has always been considered of enormous importance. It was in 1558 that an ordinance was passed (presumably at Diane's instigation) to the effect that every publisher should present to the libraries of Blois and Fontainebleau a copy of each book he issued. This copy-tax soon added nearly eight hundred volumes to the national collection. All of Diane's books are marked with an ambiguous cipher, cleverly arranged to represent what might be taken for the initials of Henry and his queen, Catherine de Medici, or Henry and his mistress. This was very far-sighted of Diane, who wished to avoid offending this powerful de Medici, a most distinguished collector herself.

The origin of the devices on the covers of Diane de Poitiers' books is interesting. When first a widow she ordered each volume stamped with a laurel springing from a tomb, and the motto, 'I live alone in grief.' But later, when Henry offered his consolation, she suppressed both the tomb and the legend. Her famous crescent shone not only on her books, but on the palace walls of France, in the Louvre, at Fontainebleau and Anet. Her initials, so conspicuous on her breviaries, were not absent either from that little treasury of books which she and Henry II assembled in the Château d'Anet. Her boudoir was renowned, not only for its luxurious size, its fine furniture, exquisite paintings, and gorgeous tapestries designed by Bernard Van Orley, but for a cabinet of delightful volumes. Oddly enough, this literary trove was not discovered until long after the owners ceased to be. The bedchamber did not relinquish its secret, and the cache remained unnoticed until the death of the Princess de Condé in 1723.

One of the most beautiful volumes from her library was sold in the collection of the Marquess of Lothian in 1932. It was her own copy of Boccaccio's 'de la louenge et vertu des nobles et clares dames,' printed in Paris by Anthoine Vérard in 1493. Bound in dark olive morocco, the back and sides decorated with gilt arabesque borders, with the interlaced initials of Diane, and her bows, quivers, and crescents, it sold for ninety-four hundred dollars to a New York collector.

The vivacious Diane lives in the pages of Clément Marot, Ronsard, Du Bellay, and other poets. Her château at Anet was justly celebrated, combining the great talents of such famous French artists as Philippe Delorme who built it, Jean Goujon who carved it, and Jean Cousin who made the mirrors. Leonard Limousin furnished the enamels, and Bernard de Palissy supplied the furnishings. Let wealthy collectors yearn for the gorgeous trappings by

Goujon, Limousin, and the rest — give me the contents of Diane's little cabinet!

For Americans it is interesting to note that among the Bibles, psalm-books, discourses on sibyls, and other items in Diane de Poitiers' library, were two books relating to this country, Serveto's edition of Ptolemy's Geography, published at Lyons in 1541, and 'Singularitez de la France Antarctique,' printed by Christopher Plantin at Antwerp in 1558. And so a woman has the distinction of being one of the earliest collectors of Americana.

Queen Isabella of Spain, the patroness of Columbus, was an ardent book-lover. I longed for years to own a volume from her library and that of her neglected husband Ferdinand. Nearly all of them were locked up in the national libraries of Spain. I knew of one, however, in England. It was in the great collection formed by Sir Thomas Phillipps at Thirlestaone House, Cheltenham. I spent several days in that noble library, with Sir Thomas's learned grandson, Mr. T. FitzRoy Fenwick. I asked if he had a book belonging to Ferdinand and Isabella. 'Yes,' he replied, and opened a safe, taking from it a large volume bound in old green velvet.

What a book and what a provenance! It was a world-famous manuscript, 'Le Livre de La Chasse,' by Gaston de Foix, surnamed Phébus, written in the year 1387! It contained eighty-eight superb miniatures in gold and colors by an artist of superior merit, in my estimation, to the celebrated Jean Fouquet, to whom it was once attributed. Its frontispiece was a

Cy denise comment on doit chasser et prendre le loup.

T quant le
venense voul
dra chasser
le loup il :
doit enclee
ner les loups
par ceste ma
niere. premierement il doit regar
der un beau buisson. a une lieue
ou deux pres daultres grans forest.
ou il ayt beau titre de leuriers et
telle place a temoignon. et peut de
dans. et la doit tuer un cheual. ou

un buef ou autre teste grosse. et prendre
les quatre membres ansses et espau
les. et les porter et non pas traby
ner es grans forests par les quatre
parties du buysson. et que chascu
de ces quatre compaignons seront
es forests la ou enclean tout faur
son trapu. si donener abatre leur
char. et tier à la mene de leurs de
uantr. et ampner par les voyes et
carrefours des forests. et puis reue
nir toulsours en trapiant iulqs
la ou la teste est morte. et laultier

'LE LIVRE DE LA CHASSE' OF GASTON DE FOIX

masterpiece, containing the device of Ferdinand and Isabella, with the arms of Castile and Aragon exquisitely emblazoned. It had been given to the 'Reyes Catolicos' by the King of France. It was beyond question the finest sporting book in the world!

When Mr. Fenwick placed it in my hands my blood-pressure must have gone up fifty points. That was in 1926. The following year I went again to see my beloved manuscript. I could not keep my mind off its charm. In 1928 I went to Cheltenham determined to possess it. I succeeded at length. The price, though high, was really low, as its value could not be measured in pounds sterling. I asked Mr. Fenwick when his grandfather had purchased it. He told me the exact date in 1828. It was precisely one hundred years *to a day*, from the time Sir Thomas Phillipps had bought it!

Queen Isabella was not only a bibliophile, but was extremely fond of the chase. It is this happy combination — books and sport — that makes this wonderful volume from her library doubly entrancing. Isabella was one of the 'women of all time.' This great manuscript is surely in the same category.

Catherine de Medici, although twenty years younger than Diane, was equally eager in her search for books. It was her good fortune to inherit the splendid tastes of her famous forbears, and she came to France bringing 'with her from Urbino a number of manuscripts that had belonged to the Eastern Emperors, and had been purchased by Cosimo de Medici.' Catherine was not so meticulous in her dealings where a book was concerned as was Cosimo. If she could secure a volume in no other way, she did not hesitate to steal it. When the Marshal Strozzi, one of her kinsmen, died in the French service, she immediately seized upon his noble library. She made no secret of the fact that she had awaited his death with anticipation, knowing that she would then be able to pounce upon the Strozzi treasures. Let us forgive her! She was a genuine bibliophile. Brantôme, in giving an account of the transaction, says most generously that the Queen purchased the books — but forgot to pay for them. She seems never to have been afraid of the natural enemies of all collectors — creditors!

A beautiful specimen from her library was sold in the Rahir sale in Paris in 1930, and brought 322,000 francs! Entitled 'La Cyropédie de Xenophon,' printed at Lyons by Jean de Tournes in 1555, it was superbly bound in citron morocco, delicately tooled in silver and gold, with the arms and devices of Catherine. In the catalogue of the sale it was described as one of the most remarkable specimens of the binder's art of the French Renaissance.

Catherine's daughter, Marguerite de Valois, Queen of Navarre, emulated the example of her distinguished mother. Nourished on books, she soon became the most learned lady of her time. Scaliger said she was liberal and studious, that she had more kingly virtues than the King. As the wife of Henry IV she collected a large library. Nearly all her books are magnificently bound and stamped with daisies, which give the volumes from her library an air of purity. Clovis Eve is said to have bound them from the Queen's own designs. Her books were systematically clad, science and philosophy in citron morocco, the poets in green, history and theology in red, Aretino in spotless white.

Anne of Austria, daughter of Philip of Spain, and wife of Louis XIII, is renowned in the kingdom of books. She was patroness of that eminent binder, Le Gascon, and the lacy gilt borders executed by him on the royal volumes are famous. Anne's library included many devotional treatises, sermons, and histories of the Church, which were no doubt recommended to her by her ecclesiastical friend, Cardinal Mazarin. The Cardinal himself was an illustrious collector, and his books have always been highly esteemed. His device, with the cardinal's hat, is frequently seen on old volumes. Anne, on the death of her husband, became Queen Mother, and for some years ruled the destinies of France. When Louis XIV reached his majority, Anne gracefully retired to the shelter of her library, where she consoled herself with her books and Mazarin.

Madame de Pompadour in her forty-three years influenced her epoch more than any other person, the King not excepted. Poets, including the great Voltaire, painters, sculptors, designers, all were indebted to her patronage. The porcelain factory at Sèvres owes its existence to her. Boucher, Fragonard, Falconnet, Cochin, each one, received from her the inspiration for his greatest works. Dérôme, one of the most skillful binders, executed his choicest coverings for her books. She was fortunate to live during an epoch in which some of the most famous illustrated volumes were issued. Madame de Pompadour was herself an illustrator and etched a set of sixty-two plates, which she presented to her friends. Her most famous work was her etched frontispiece, after Boucher, for Corneille's 'Rodogune,' published in 1760. Amateurs with a curious perversity prefer the rather naughty volumes of Madame de Pompadour to the austere books of Madame de Maintenon.

Madame de Montespan's love for Louis XIV is well known, but her love of books is seldom dwelt upon by historians. She became the beloved of the King in 1668, and lived during a period that saw the rise of Corneille and Molière, and the development of book illustration with copperplate engravings. But a few works from her library remain, one of them, a copy of the Psalms of David, in seven volumes, was printed especially for her use. Luckily, an extremely interesting volume survives, the Marquise de Montespan's own copy of the 'Works of an Author Aged Seven' (her son, the young Duc de Maine), published under the direction of his governess, Madame de Maintenon, in 1678.

This leads me to her successor in royal favor, none other than the poor governess Frances, afterward the Marquise de Maintenon, second wife of Louis XIV. The Grand Monarch insisted, with pleasing propriety, that all the ladies surrounding him should be lovers of books. While Madame de Maintenon's

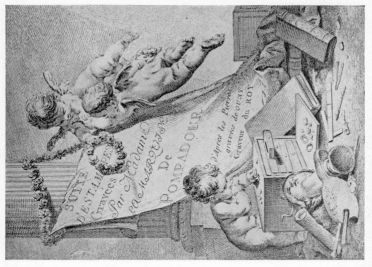

FRONTISPIECE TO A SERIES OF ENGRAVINGS BY
MADAME DE POMPADOUR

MADAME DE POMPADOUR IN HER
LIBRARY

name is also a household word, few have even peeped
into her library at Saint-Cyr. The bindings are
magnificent, and the gold is in profusion, but the contents of the volumes are decidedly ordinary, dull
works of theology, philosophy, sermons, concord-
ances. The more mundane volumes of that period are
conspicuously absent.

The Queen Marie Antoinette was also a book-
collector, and the volumes from her library are all
highly treasured. I had the good fortune to own her
own copy of 'Les Baisers' of Dorat, one of the most
beautiful books of the eighteenth century. It is in
green morocco, with the Queen's arms in gold on the
sides. It is now in the collection of Mr. Joseph
Widener.

The most touching relic of this unfortunate lady
is her own prayer-book. When she entered the
Prison of the Conciergerie for the last time, she
clasped tightly in her white hands the 'Office de la
Divine Providence,' by Pierre Préault, 1757. A few
hours before her execution, in deepest anguish she
wrote on the fly-leaf:

> 16 October (1793). Half past four o'clock in the
> morning. My God, have pity on me! My eyes have
> no more tears to shed for you, my poor children Adieu.
> Adieu.
>
> Marie-Antoinette

This tender volume, an ever-living memorial of
the Revolution, was long in the possession of M.
Garinet, who left his splendid library to his native
city, Châlons-sur-Marne.

When I purchased *en bloc* the Roederer library in Paris in 1923, there was one little volume that I particularly desired. It was Moreau's catalogue of Marie Antoinette's own library, entitled, 'Bibliothèque de Madame la Dauphine,' printed in 1770. It has a gracious frontispiece, exquisitely engraved by Eisen, representing Marie Antoinette as Dauphine being crowned by the Graces. What made this charming volume so enticing was that it was bound in old red morocco with the arms of her husband, later to become Louis XVI.

The world, I am told, has become tired of kings and of royalty, so perhaps you are wearying of a too vigorous flow of purple blood. I must therefore turn to a woman who was a genuine collector, with just enough spice in her nature to make her eternally attractive. Madame de Verrue was born in 1670, and at thirteen years of age espoused the Comte de Verrue, a noble of considerable wealth. She was a person of charm, of beauty, and of distinction, as can be perceived from her portrait by Largillière. Her husband died in 1703, and whatever emotions she may have felt for him she now directed to book-collecting. Indeed, almost overnight she sprouted as a real collector. Some contemporary said of her that, fearing to take a chance on heaven, Madame de Verrue determined to have a good time here below. Her epitaph is famous:

Here lies in sleep secure a dame inclined to mirth
Who, by way of making sure, chose her Paradise on earth.

MARIE ANTOINETTE'S COPY OF 'LES BAISERS' OF DORAT

She had countless love-affairs, famous in her time, and gathered many books even more renowned, and, a woman of rare judgment, she chose to collect the masterpieces of the world's literature. French collectors, with their debonair manner, now prefer among her volumes the trifles that bear such names as 'Gallant Adventures at the Court of France,' the 'Love-Affairs of the Grand Monarch with Mademoiselle du Tron,' the 'Parnasse Satyrique,' and many other choice *morceaux*, which are really tame in comparison with some of the novels of today. Madame de Verrue had her own librarian, and left for the edification of posterity an inventory of all her property. Her taste was sure, exquisite, unfailing. She possessed the finest pictures by Van Dyke, Rubens, Rembrandt, and Nattier. Everything she had was according to the best canons of all time. Her snuff-boxes in gold, in tortoise-shell, in porcelain, in lacquer, in jasper, defied computation. Among the most interesting things in the inventory is the catalogue of snuffs, more than sixty-five in number, which filled these delicate boxes, so prettily carried by Madame de Verrue. The snuff goes by vintages. For instance, there is a special cask dated 1734, a box marked 1736, another given her by the Cardinal de Rohan in 1740. There were five boxes of 'Messalina finissima,' which was kept in a leaden jar, and probably considered in the Corona-Corona class. I must reluctantly leave Madame de Verrue in the fragrant odor of the sweetest tobacco.

In Paris not long ago, Baroness James de Rothschild passed away at the age of eighty-three. The owner of the finest private library in France, she was the dean of modern women book collectors.

France is naturally proud of her lady book-lovers. They created a noble history, extending from the early part of the fifteenth century, which encompassed all the grace, the *esprit*, the elegance of times long past. I may perhaps have treated them too openly. I would not, if I could, paint them as saints. They would be the first to rebuke me. We love them for their many-sided characters, their enchanting ways, their charming wit, and above all for their love of books.

Quentin Bauchart has written a delightful treatise entitled 'Les Femmes Bibliophiles de France' (1886), and Andrew Lang has a charming essay on the same subject.

No country in the world has had so many great collectors as England. Her heritage is a glorious one. Henry VII, the founder of the house of Tudor, became a collector of printed books and manuscripts, though his taste was apparently not shared by his wife, Elizabeth, eldest daughter of Edward IV. His son Henry VIII inherited his father's tastes, and at least three of his wives were able to share his enthusiasms and collected their own libraries, having their books specially bound for them. Books from the libraries of Catherine of Aragon, Anne Boleyn, and Katherine Parr, with their arms impressed on the bindings, are all to be found in the old Royal Library in the British Museum.

Both the Tudor princesses, daughters of King Henry VIII, were book-collectors, and the library of the unhappy woman known to posterity as 'Bloody Mary' was deposited in the British Museum in 1757. It is a notable collection, the books for the most part having been bound for the Queen by Thomas Berthelet, the royal binder.

One of the most outstanding book-collectors of Queen Elizabeth's day was a woman as celebrated as Elizabeth herself, but alas, far less fortunate. I refer to her tragic kinswoman, Mary Queen of Scots. This romantic princess, famous for her beauty and her talent as well as for her misfortunes, was a great bibliophile. Her love of books may have been inherited from her father James V, whose library was sacked by English invaders. It was certainly encouraged in France, where she lived at a time when the examples of Catherine de Medici and Diane de Poitiers had made the possession of a library fashionable.

Mary's taste was by no means narrow and her son James VI, when he inherited her library at Holyrood, found books to delight the heart of any collector. The works of Rabelais, Marguerite de Navarre, and most of the great French poets; romances of chivalry; tales of voyage and discovery; religious books, including books of hours; manuscripts on vellum; books in Greek and Latin — and of these it may be mentioned to her credit that she wished to bequeath them to the University of Saint Andrews; all these and many more testified to the literary discrimination of one of the loveliest and most tragic figures in the history of the world.

The bindings of her books show in part her sad and pitiful history. Many of them are black and have black edges — a mark of mourning for her first husband, the Dauphin of France, who shortly after their marriage became King Francis II, but who died after only two years of married life. These books have impressed in the sides a cipher — M and F — for Marie and François, with the crown of France and the motto, 'Sa vertu M'atire,' an anagram on the name Marie Stuarte.

Queen Elizabeth, too, loved books. As a young princess exiled from court, she amused herself by embroidering bindings for her own volumes, on blue silk with gold and silver thread, in the style made famous a few years later by the nuns of Little Gidding. After she became the mighty Queen, she established her own library at Whitehall, and in her day this must have been the finest cabinet of presentation books in the universe. Unhappily many of them are lost, but it takes only a slight effort of the imagination to see the manuscripts of Sir Philip Sidney, of Sir Walter Raleigh, and of the unfortunate Earl of Leicester, all presented to her by their noble authors. The 'Tales of Hemetes the Heremyte,' 1576, by George Gascoigne, has an engraving of the author, meekly kneeling upon his knees, presenting a copy of his book to his royal patroness.

Edmund Spenser dedicated to Queen Elizabeth 'The Faerie Queene,' with the finest lines ever prefaced to a work:

> To the most high, mightie, and magnificent Em-
> peresse, renouned for pietie, vertue, and all gra-
> cious government: Elizabeth by the Grace of
> God, Queene of England, France, and Ireland,
> and of Virginia, Defender of the Faith &c.
> Her most humble Servaunt, Edmund Spenser,
> doth in all humilitie dedicate, present, and con-
> secrate these his labours, to live with the eternitie
> of her Fame.

Perhaps William Shakespeare gave her the manuscript with a dutiful dedication of his Sonnets, or his
most popular play, 'Romeo and Juliet,' which she
doubtless read with much enjoyment. In the British
Museum, in the Bodleian, and in the Pierpont Morgan Library some of the treasures of the great Queen
can still be seen, the royal arms emblazoned in gold
on their luxurious liveries. Queen Elizabeth not only
collected the rare and splendid books of her immortal
contemporaries, but she gathered about her person
the great poets and dramatists themselves, and by
her encouragement and inspiration fostered an era
whose brilliance has never been equaled.

The poets of England, however, had a patroness
whom they loved far more than the imperious Elizabeth. The Countess of Pembroke, 'Sidney's Sister,
Pembroke's Mother,' had in some respects a much
stronger hold upon the literary imagination of her
time. She was the Urania of Spenser's 'Colin Clout,'
and she suggested the composition of her brother's
'Arcadia,' which she edited and augmented. In fact,
Sir Philip Sidney called his celebrated romance, not

'The Arcadia,' but 'The Countess of Pembroke's Arcadia.'

Her own copy of this great work, which she gave to her daughter, the Countess of Montgomery, is one of the treasures in the library at Harvard College. A neat story hangs upon this precious volume. I had always known of its existence. Even in my youthful days I coveted it in the library of Mr. Clarence S. Bement, of Philadelphia, one of the most fastidious collectors of his time. My mouth used to water as I tenderly took it in my hands, to admire one of the finest bindings of the Elizabethan period. In contemporary red morocco, the back and sides are powdered with small hearts and flames impressed in gold; in the center are the initials of the houses of Sidney and Montgomery. The inscription, signed by the Earl of Ancram, is written on the title-page, 'This was the Countess of Pembroke's own book given me by the Countess of Montgomery her daughter, 1625.'

Some years later, with the book-hunter's proverbial luck, I acquired this magnificent volume. I showed it to poor Harry Widener, then just beginning to form his great collection. Tears came to his eyes when he first saw it. 'Take it,' I said. 'It belongs to you of right.' 'No,' he said firmly but sorrowfully, 'I cannot afford it now, and I must always be able to pay for any book I buy.' I reluctantly sold it to someone else.

After five more years the bibliophile's god decreed that the book should once again come into my possession. I wrapped it carefully and rushed with it to Mr. Widener. Before I had a chance to open my package he said, 'I know what you have brought me. It is the Countess of Pembroke's own Arcadia.' It is now in his library in the Harry Elkins Widener Memorial, at Harvard.

By a happy coincidence, the library of the greatest of all American women collectors rests in the same building. Miss Amy Lowell was an inspired bibliophile with a restless imagination, great courage and untiring zeal, those disquieting qualities of the astute book-lover. I have known her to travel miles just to see a fine book.

I remember as though it were yesterday one day years ago when Miss Lowell, accompanied by her dear friend Mrs. Ada Russell, the noted actress, visited me in Philadelphia. Miss Lowell was eager to see the original draft of one of Keats's poems. That evening we sat down to rather a formal dinner at eight o'clock. But at ten minutes after eight all formality had entirely disappeared. I recall Eddie Newton was in particularly good form that evening. Between courses, in which Miss Lowell indulged in large fat cigars, for she was as fond of tobacco as Madame Verrue, we had a lively discussion as to which was the first draft of Keats's beautiful sonnet 'On First Looking into Chapman's Homer,' her own, or the one in the Pierpont Morgan Library.

Miss Lowell had her own way, as usual. Then she really started something. She stated that there was a vital quality in modern verse found lacking in the old. She donned her war-paint and prepared for the fray. For opponent she had that veteran of many battles, Joseph Pennell. He, naturally, championed the other side, and the battle raged eloquent and heated for hours. The timid ones were speechless, while others tried unsuccessfully to interpose a few feeble blows. The food had long since been cleared away, the wine-glasses alone remaining upon the table. Suddenly Miss Lowell exclaimed: 'I'm dying of hunger. It's four-thirty — time for something to eat!' I routed out the cook, who sleepily but adequately fed the famished book-lovers, most of them for the first time in their lives breakfasting by the light of the rising sun. I can yet recall Miss Lowell, going down the stairs on the way to her hotel, still arguing with Joseph Pennell.

Miss Lowell had a well-defined plan in the formation of her library. She wanted unpublished Keats material first and foremost, and the Keats manuscripts in her collection speak more eloquently of her successful endeavors than anything I can say of her. If she desired a particular item, she would not rest until she secured it. It was not unusual for her to call me from Boston at any hour of the night to learn if I had purchased something for her at one of the auction sales. The cost was nothing, the book everything.

Another great woman collector of books lived in Brooklyn, New York, which has the proud distinction of having had more distinguished bibliophiles than any other city of its size in the world. I refer to the late Mrs. Norton Quincy Pope, who gathered together in a short time a magnificent collection.

AMY LOWELL

Among her treasures she possessed probably the finest Caxton in the world, a dream of a book, the only perfect copy in existence of Malory's 'Morte d'Arthur,' printed at Westminster in 1485. At her death it passed first to Robert Hoe, and then into the Pierpont Morgan Library.

This reference to the Morgan collection must inevitably bring up the name of its distinguished director, Miss Belle da Costa Greene, who has reached a height in the world of books that no other woman has ever attained. Miss Greene, besides possessing a genuine love of books, has a knowledge of customs and manners in the mediaeval period excelled by few scholars.

It is sometimes dangerous for women to possess rare volumes — they might for that very reason receive offers of marriage! This sounds fantastic, but it is true. I can only quote the celebrated case of a great feminine amateur at the beginning of the nineteenth century. Miss Richardson Currer owned a valuable library containing over fifteen thousand volumes, including a beautiful copy printed on vellum of the 'Book of St. Albans',' 1496, written by the first woman sports writer, Dame Juliana Berners. Richard Heber, probably the most enthusiastic book-collector who ever lived, tried to wheedle it out of her by hook or crook. Not succeeding by nefarious ways, he took the honorable method of proposing marriage. The lady, not caring to share the volume with a husband, indignantly refused. Good for her!

A charming American lady has recently acquired

the superb Pembroke copy of the first edition of the
'Book of St. Albans',' as the 'Book of Hawking and
Hunting' is usually termed, printed in 1486. It is ten
years earlier than the romantic copy that belonged
to Miss Currer. I would rather have the first issue
of this famous book than the one on which Mr.
Heber looked with such longing eyes, even if it were
printed on vellum. It is particularly fitting that this
famous volume, written by a woman, should grace
the shelves of a distinguished feminine collector.

There have been two women who by their bookish
gifts are enshrined in the hearts of all bibliophiles.
In 1892 a widow, unknown to fame but not to fortune,
walked into a bookstore in London and stated almost
casually that she would like to buy the finest private
library then in existence, the renowned collection of
Lord Spencer, at Althorp. The bookseller stood
aghast. After he recovered from the shock, he replied that Earl Spencer would never part with his
precious library. The lady, nothing daunted, walked
into another shop. Here she was more warmly received and, although the dealer had not the slightest
reason to know that the Earl would sell his library,
he politely informed her that he would write to his
lordship. The negotiations were successful and the
lady drew a check for over two hundred thousand
pounds in payment, the largest sum, up to that time,
that had been given for a collection of books and
manuscripts. Who was this courageous lady? It was
none other than Mrs. John Rylands, of Manchester,
England, who presented the Spencer library to that

BELLE DA COSTA GREENE

city as a memorial to her husband. This gift placed Manchester at once on the map as a center for learning and scholarship. This, in the annals of book-collecting, is one of the finest gifts made by man or woman.

The other lady to whom I referred above happily lives in America. Mrs. Edward S. Harkness has made extraordinary gifts to American institutions, and when she presented the Melk copy of the Gutenberg Bible to Yale University she made a sensation on two continents.

The West is now rivaling the East in feminine activities in the 'City of Books,' to use a phrase of Anatole France. Mrs. Edward L. Doheny in Los Angeles has beautiful specimens of typography and many exquisite bindings and manuscripts. Some literary treasures of the highest importance are in the library of Mrs. W. H. Stark, of Orange, Texas. Mrs. F. M. P. Taylor has just presented a Fine Arts Center to Colorado Springs, and her collections contain beautiful specimens of some of the rarest English books.

I have always thought it rather strange that no wife of a President of the United States has been a book-collector. A few were interested in books to read, but not to collect. It is a sad commentary.

There have been mighty women book-hunters. There will be many more in the future, for the quest has everything that appeals to woman — mystery, charm, subtlety, sweet companionship. It has just enough spice in it to make it eternally attractive. Ladies, why leave the triumphs of this sport to Men?

VI

THE LIBRARIES
OF THE PRESIDENTS OF
THE UNITED STATES

THE degree of greatness of each of the Presidents of
the United States can be determined by his interest
in literature and in books. What the Presidents read
and the contents of their libraries make an interesting
study.[1] Most of the great names in American history
were true lovers of books and liked to have them
always at their side. Benjamin Franklin was a great
collector and purchased rare books as early as 1732
for the Library Company of Philadelphia. Other
great men who never reached the Presidency were
also collectors; we cannot dwell upon them, but must
confine ourselves to the bookish activities of the
Presidents themselves.

The first President of the United States was a true
collector. Washington was born in Virginia and had,
when a youth, as his near neighbor, William Byrd of

[1] I am indebted to my dear friend, Doctor Clarence S. Brigham,
Director of the American Antiquarian Society, for much of the material
relating to presidential bookplates and the present location of presidential libraries. His enthusiasm for the subject of this paper was con-
tagious and his collaboration has made the writing of it a real pleasure.
All the Presidents' bookplates are illustrated in my article in the *Proceedings of the American Antiquarian Society* (1935).

CLARENCE S. BRIGHAM

Westover, the first man in the American Colonies
who formed a great library. There were many fine
collections in the great estates that were within a
day's ride of Mount Vernon. In fact, this section of
the country was the center of the culture of the time.
While the New England Provinces had scholars of no
mean ability, and collectors to boot, the main interest
was in theology and dialectics, the austere Mather
influence prevailing. The broader European culture
was current in Virginia and the College of William
and Mary had a liberalizing influence throughout the
Colony. Washington came under this influence early.
He was a man of considerable means and delighted in
his library, owning the best editions of his favorite
authors.

Washington had his own binder in Philadelphia
and many of the volumes from his library were bound
in calf, tooled on the back with emblematical designs.
Addison and Goldsmith were the authors he liked
best, although he delved into Shakespeare, Swift,
Smollett, Sterne, and Fielding. As with many another great man, Cervantes was a prime favorite and
he enjoyed reading 'Don Quixote.' In fact, he had
two copies of Doctor Smollett's translation of 'Don
Quixote' published in London in four volumes in 1786.
For one of the copies we know that on September 17,
1787, Washington paid twenty-two shillings and
sixpence.

Washington was naturally interested in the classics
of the eighteenth century and possessed copies of
'Chesterfield's Letters,' 'The Adventures of Tele-

machus,' Fielding's 'Tom Jones,' Pope's 'Works,' in six volumes, Smollett's 'Humphry Clinker,' 'The Beauties of Sterne,' Voltaire's 'Letters,' 'Gulliver's Travels,' and Gibbon's 'Decline and Fall of the Roman Empire.' He also possessed a copy of Doctor Johnson's Dictionary in two large volumes published in London in 1786. It was appraised in 1800 for ten dollars.

The President's wife was also interested in books. We find that Mrs. Washington had among her treasures 'The Jilts, or Female Fortune Hunters,' which bears upon the title-page the following autograph:

Mrs. Martha Washington Her Book 1774.

This was purchased, however, twenty-two years after she had plighted her troth to George and, therefore, the subject-matter of the book was of little use to her.

Washington delighted in buying books about his native State, and among the prized volumes in the Boston Athenaeum is Washington's copy of Beverley's 'History of Virginia, 1722,' with his signature and date, 1769, written boldly upon the title-page.

A great many of Washington's books were sold in Philadelphia in 1876 by M. Thomas & Sons, Auctioneers. Among them was one labeled 'Virginia Journal' and consisted of many pamphlets relating to Virginia and printed in Williamsburg, the State Capital. It had been bound for Washington and bore his name with a mighty flourish upon the title-page.

My uncle, Moses Polock, was present at the sale and bought this volume for the huge sum of twenty-two dollars, one of the highest prices at the sale.

Washington, as is well known, was interested in agriculture. He was the first farmer of his day. He corresponded with Arthur Young, James Anderson, and other famous agriculturists of England. The book from which Washington laid out the gardens at Mount Vernon recently came into my possession. It is entitled 'New Principles of Gardening,' by Batty Langley, London, 1728. It bears on the title-page the signature of George Washington, 1761, 'Cost Sterling 15 shillings.' When the inventory of the library of Washington was made after his death this volume was appraised at the magnificent sum of two dollars. It is a quarto volume, beautifully illustrated with copper plates, with plans and layouts of formal gardens. We can imagine Washington, with painstaking care, reading these new principles and putting them into practical execution in the gardens of his lovely home along the slopes of the Potomac.

Washington, like all book-collectors, and to the despair of booksellers, was anxious to make advantageous purchases, and enjoyed buying them at appraised, rather than market prices. When the Custis estate was being settled he wrote, 'I had no particular reason for keeping, and handing down to his son, the books of the late Col. Custis, saving that I thought it would be taking the advantage of a low appraisement to make them my own property.' We would all like to buy the books of George Washington at their appraised value in 1800! Washington states in his diary that he visited the shop of John Bradford in Philadelphia and purchased books and pamphlets relating to the controversy between Great Britain and the Colonies.

Washington was naturally interested in works on military science, of which he had many. There were numerous volumes on the art of war, on the Prussian evolutions, on military discipline, on fortifications, and on appointments to the army. He read these faithfully, and occasionally there is a pointed note on the margins.

Toward the end of the eighteenth century the world became interested in aviation. Washington was no exception. In the inventory of his estate it is recorded that he owned, at the time of his death, a copy of Doctor Jeffries' 'Narrative of the Two Aerial Voyages with Monsieur Blanchard,' London, 1786. It is a fascinating account of the first crossing from England to France by air. Only last year this very copy was offered for sale and I secured it. It bears on the title-page the boldest and finest signature of Washington I have ever seen.

Washington, apart from being a book-collector, was also a collector of choice wines and liquors. As a hospitable host he liked to secure the rarest and finest vintages. Nothing delighted him more than to place before his guests some exquisite old liquor, which had arrived by packet from France. Knowing his taste for such things, I was very anxious to secure a volume entitled 'Cordial for Low Spirits' which I

A
NARRATIVE

OF THE

TWO AERIAL VOYAGES

OF

DOCTOR JEFFRIES WITH MONS. BLANCHARD;

WITH

METEOROLOGICAL OBSERVATIONS AND REMARKS.

THE FIRST VOYAGE, ON THE THIRTIETH OF NOVEMBER, 1784,
FROM LONDON INTO KENT:

THE SECOND, ON THE SEVENTH OF JANUARY, 1785,
FROM ENGLAND INTO FRANCE.

BY DOCTOR JEFFRIES.

PRESENTED TO THE ROYAL SOCIETY, APRIL 14, 1785;
AND READ BEFORE THEM, JANUARY, 1786.

LONDON:
PRINTED FOR THE AUTHOR;
AND SOLD BY J. ROBSON, NEW BOND-STREET

M.DCC.LXXXVI.

GEORGE WASHINGTON'S COPY, WITH ONE OF HIS
FINEST AND LARGEST SIGNATURES HERE SHOWN
IN REDUCED SIZE

knew he at the time possessed. I remembered seeing Washington's copy offered in a bookseller's catalogue in Boston and I immediately telegraphed for it. When the volume arrived, instead of finding in it recipes for enlivening old cordials, such as chartreuse and benedictine, you may imagine my disappointment in discovering that it consisted entirely of religious and moral precepts, not at all calculated to raise low spirits.

Washington not only kept his volumes in the study at Mount Vernon, but many were placed in a beautiful bookcase in the dining-room. The family and heirs of the First President gradually dispersed the volumes, and now they are scattered far and wide. The largest collection of them is in the Boston Athenaeum, which in 1848 purchased 455 volumes and about 750 pamphlets. The price paid was $3800, which even in those days was considered a bargain.

The inventory of Washington's library made at the time of his death listed 884 volumes, exclusive of pamphlets and maps. The original inventory is missing from the records at Fairfax Court House, but is known from a copy sent by John A. Washington to Edward Everett, and is published in Everett's 'Life of Washington,' 1860. (Also printed with additional details in the Boston Athenaeum Catalogue of the Washington Collection.)

Washington's library under his will went to his favorite nephew, Judge Bushrod Washington, who added to it many volumes of his own, about doubling the size of the collection. Upon his death in 1826, he left 468 miscellaneous volumes to his nephew, John A. Washington, and 658 miscellaneous volumes, 1125 miscellaneous pamphlets, besides 169 volumes of State Papers, 22 volumes of Journals of Congress, and 649 volumes of law books, to his nephew, George C. Washington. The last three lots were destined for Bushrod Washington Herbert, the son of a niece, in case he should be trained for the law.

The books left to George C. Washington, or what remained of them, were sold about 1847 to Henry Stevens of London and in the following year were purchased through the raising of a subscription of about four thousand dollars, for the Boston Athenaeum. Of the books so purchased, 354 volumes and about 450 pamphlets came from the original George Washington library, and 80 volumes and about 300 pamphlets belonged to Bushrod Washington or other members of the family. Speaking of the books from Washington's library, the Report of the Library for 1849 quaintly remarks, 'They would be regarded even in Europe as curiosities of great interest and value, and would command prices which might seem incredible to one unacquainted with sums given for objects associated with the memory of highly distinguished men.'

The books which Bushrod Washington left to his nephew, John A. Washington, finally passed to the latter's grandson, Lawrence Washington of Alexandria, and gradually came upon the market between 1876 and 1892. The largest lot, containing 138 titles, was sold by Mr. Thomas & Sons at Philadelphia in 1876, the price being very low, less than two thousand dollars for the whole collection. From 1890 to 1892, Stan. V. Henkels held several sales which included many books from Washington's library and where high prices for the first time were realized. Since that time scarcely a year has passed but a volume or two from Washington's library has come up at public auction, the prices steadily increasing until within recent years any authentic book with his autograph or bookplate has brought at least two thousand dollars, and many have brought much more.

The record price at auction for a book from Washington's library was realized this year. In January, 1936, Washington's own copy of his 'Official Letters to the Honorable American Congress,' 1795, two volumes in the original bindings, sold for ninety-eight hundred dollars. I did not hesitate to give this price. It is considered the most desirable of all books from his library.

The best account of his library is contained in the Boston Athenaeum's splendid 'Catalogue of the Washington Collection,' compiled by A. P. C. Griffin and W. C. Lane in 1897. A few items of additional interest can be found in the Reverend Eliphalet N. Potter's 'Washington a Model in his Library and Life,' 1895.

Washington's bookplate appears in many, but not all, of the genuine volumes from his library. In the Boston Athenaeum list, 137 volumes out of 884 contain the bookplate. When he obtained it, or how he used it, or when he discontinued its use, cannot be told from a study of the volumes in which it was inserted. Nor is there any clue to the engraver. Richard C. Lichtenstein thought that it was made between 1777 and 1781, and, because of the incorrectness of its heraldry, by an American engraver. Charles Dexter Allen thought that from its appearance it was engraved in England about 1770. An examination of Washington's carefully kept accounts does not reveal any entry for expense of a bookplate.

The original copper-plate was owned in the family as late as 1861, and from it many restrikes were made at different times, distinguishable from the original in the quality of the paper. In the American Antiquarian Society collection, in addition to the original bookplate, there are a dozen restrikes. One of these has penned on the reverse: 'An impression from the original Copper of Gen'l Washington's bookplate; given to me by L. W. Washington November 1861, and by me to Mr. Etting. B. M. (Brantz Mayer).' Another has 'Taken from the original plate, and presented to H. S. Shurtleff by Mr. Hazeltine of Philadelphia Oct. 2, 1868.' Another, undated, has 'From original plate in possession of Wᵐ Alexʳ Smith, N. Y., rec'd by him from Geo. L. Washington, of Charlestown, W. Va.' A restrike sold at Merwin-Clayton's, March 1, 1907, states that it was 'Presented to Col. Henry J. Hunt in Feby 1861, by Mrs. Lewis Washington, at her house near Harper's Ferry, Va., as certified by Col. Hunt. The original plate was at this time owned by and in the possession of Lewis Washington.' C. D. Allen stated in 1894 that the late James Eddy Mauran of Newport knew the man who owned the copper and that, after making a few restrikes, this man, fearing other restrikes would be made, cut the copper in pieces and threw it into the Schuylkill River. In spite of this story, the original copper was saved, and the owner, William Alexander Smith, presented it in 1907 to the Metropolitan Museum of Fine Arts in New York. Another original early copper, engraved after this same design, came into my possession several years ago.

There are also re-engraved forgeries of the plate, several of which were inserted in a collection of nearly two hundred books sold at a sale conducted at Washington, D.C., March 9, 1863, by W. L. Wall & Co. The forgery was so poorly executed that the volumes were readily seen to be spurious and brought very low prices.

Books from the library of George Washington represent more than historical curiosities. When examining them, and looking over the catalogue of his books, we get an insight into his character that is not revealed in his biographies.

The second President, John Adams, had one of the largest libraries in the Colonies. He was a graduate of Harvard College, and was interested in books from the time he was a student at Cambridge until his death. He, like Washington, was interested in works on the eighteenth century and collected Voltaire and others, but Fielding, Smollett, and Burns were strangely missing from his collection. Cervantes and Shakespeare were in his library, however.

John Adams's library contained many of the Greek and Latin classics, such as 'Plato's Works' in three volumes, published in Paris in 1578, and the 'Works of Aristotle,' published in Paris in 1629. He also had early editions of Bacon, Cardinal Bembo, Diderot, Frederick the Great, John Locke, Isaac Newton, and others. A duller list of books I have never seen than the catalogue of John Adams's library. It consisted of many books which no gentleman's library should be without. This was, in the eighteenth century, an unfortunate admission. The lighter side of literature is sadly wanting. He had a copy of Johnson's 'Lives of the English Poets,' but there was no 'Rasselas' nor any of the imaginative works of the great lexicographer.

John Adams had some excellent Americana, including tracts of the highest degree of rarity; among them are Winslow's 'Good News from New England,' 1634, and Joseph Warren's 'Oration on the Boston Massacre, 1772,' which was presented to him by General Warren.

There are several volumes of Americana in the Adams library which at one time belonged to the Reverend Thomas Prince, one of the earliest collectors in Massachusetts, who bequeathed them to his old church in Boston. Two of the Adams lot contain the bookplate of the Old South Library. John Adams appreciated the books of Thomas Prince; how much, the following narrative will explain. Adams wrote on October 23, 1811: 'I mounted up to the balcony of Dr. Sewall's church where was assembled a collection which Mr. Prince had devoted himself to make in the twentieth year of his age. Such a treasure never existed anywhere else and can never again be made.' In the catalogue of John Adams's library issued by the Trustees of the Public Library of the City of Boston, 1917, there is the following illuminating note: 'It seems probable that on one or more of his visits to this balcony Mr. Adams borrowed these volumes and failed to return them.' From this I must admit that he had a proper appreciation of the great rarities in the Prince collection.

John Adams was a constant collector of books throughout his life. Living to an age of over ninety years, he spent much of the latter part of his life in reading books on learned or abstruse subjects, many in foreign languages, and always for the improvement of his mind. In 1822, when in his eighty-seventh year, he presented to the town of Quincy what he termed the 'fragments' of his library, reserving only a few volumes for the consolation of his waning days. Probably some of his books had been given to children and friends, yet the library remained pretty much in its entirety. It contained 2756 volumes, one of the largest libraries in New England at that time. One of his conditions was that a catalogue should be printed, which was done in 1823. Since the library could not be cared for adequately and, in fact, some volumes were stolen, and since the nature of the books made them of little use to a small community, the town of Quincy turned over the collection in 1893 to the Boston Public Library. In 1917 a catalogue of the collection was published, containing nearly three hundred additional titles received from various members of the Adams family since John Adams's death.

John Adams's bookplate was an armorial plate, with the arms of the Boylston family, bordered by a garter with a quotation from Tacitus and the whole surrounded by thirteen stars. Charles Francis Adams, in the Massachusetts Historical Society Proceedings, Series 2, volume 2, page 84, gives an account of the bookplate, stating that the general idea of the plate, with the motto and the stars, was in the design of a seal for the United States which John Adams had planned in 1776, but which was not finally adopted; also that the plate was engraved by Carpenter of London in 1785 or 1786 and the original copper had been lost. There are, however, photographic reproductions on modern paper.

There are other plates carrying the name of John Adams, but none of these concerned the President. A woodcut plate of 'John Adams's Library,' which was printed at Hudson, New York, was owned by a member of a Scotch family living in Columbia County, New York. Another plate, 'John Adams, His Book, 17—,' is rudely engraved by I. Cunningham and is of another family. There were thirty-seven John Adamses listed as heads of families in the Massachusetts Census of 1790. A third John Adams plate, armorial with the arms consisting of a star centered in a cross, is undoubtedly English.

1 A Caution on the present contest between France & G. Britain
2 Impartial review of the causes & principles of the Fr. revolution
3 Independance des Americains des E.U. par Griffith.
4 Nicholas's speech on the bill concernᵍ elections of Presidᵗ & V.P.
5 Gallatin's speech on the foreign intercourse bill.
6 Addison's observations on Gallatin's speech
7 Addison on liberty of speech & of the Press.
8 Message of the President on the mission of Pinckney, Marshal, & Gerry.
9 Logan on the Natural & Social order of the world.
10 Gallatin's speech above mentᵈ with an additional note.
11 Dissent of the minority of the H. of R. of Penna on the address to the Presdᵗ.
12 Enquiry into the Sedition law.
13 Addison's charge to the Grand jury.
14 Debates of Virginia delegates on the Alien & Sedition laws.
15 Proceedings of the Virginia assembly on answers of the states on dᵒ
16 Thompson's letters to Curtius.
17 Martin's Scene to the play of Columbus.
18 Ogden's Appeal on the religion & Politics of Connecticut.
19 ———— view of the Calvinistic clubs.
20 Criminal law of Virginia.

AN INDEX IN JEFFERSON'S AUTOGRAPH IN A BOOK FROM HIS
LIBRARY

Thomas Jefferson, third President of the United States, was a book-collector in every sense of the word. He had an inquisitive mind, something like Benjamin Franklin's, and he liked to secure first-hand information from original sources. Jefferson bought books on art, literature, religion, architecture, philosophy, chemistry, husbandry — in fact, on almost every subject. He corresponded with the great men of his time, and, although a politician, was interested in many things besides politics. When he built Monticello he wanted to have therein the best books, not only of the ancient world, the great classics of European literature, but the works of his contemporaries and friends. He was so much interested in his library that he made a catalogue of it himself, the classification being based upon Lord Bacon's Divisions of Knowledge. In the library of the Massachusetts Historical Society is a manuscript catalogue of Jefferson's library, in which is written, '1783, Mar. 6. 2540 vols.' The catalogue extends through two hundred and thirty pages, and in the front of the book is an elaborate classification. On the third leaf is the manuscript entry: 'This mark denotes the books I have. Those unmarked I mean to procure.'

Jefferson was one of the early collectors of Americana and bought almost everything relating to the early history of this country, including some of the rarest tracts. He had these tracts bound by his own binder. Among the books were De Bry's famous collection of 'Voyages,' Purchas's 'Pilgrims,' and Smith's 'History of Virginia.'

Jefferson formed the library of the University of Virginia at Charlottesville, and he made long lists of books most desired by students. He not only was interested in the library of the University, but was its architect as well. He frequently wrote to his agents in Europe trying to secure the best books on architecture. He wanted to have the buildings at the University of Virginia practical and comfortable, but at the same time beautiful. He did not like the style of some of the University buildings in Williamsburg and states that 'buildings are often erected by individuals at considerable expense — to give these symmetry and taste would not increase their cost.' This precept was one of the wisest uttered by Jefferson, for nothing truer was ever said. He secured the great works on architecture of Inigo Jones, Vitruvius, Palladio, Gibbs, and Piranesi, and many others. Not only did he buy books on architecture, but also on interior decoration, such as Chippendale's 'Cabinet Makers Designs,' 1755, and 'Descriptions of the Houses and Gardens at Stowe,' 1783. Unfortunately many of these books were destroyed by the fire in the Library of Congress in 1851. Fire, as will be seen later, was Thomas Jefferson's special curse.

Jefferson started very young to form a collection of books. It was about the year 1760 that he began to buy books in Williamsburg, then the center of culture. Ten years later he suffered a severe loss.

In the year 1770 the house at Shadwell was destroyed by fire and Jefferson then moved to Monticello, where his preparations for a residence were rity. When this fhall be done, the government can be changed and modelled on republican principles, as may become neceffary and ufeful.

By the Conftitution it is provided, that " Nul ne peut être empêche de dire, écrire, imprimer et publier fapenfée " No one is to be impeached for expreffing, writing or printing his thoughts.

This provifion is abfolutely neceffary to a free country, but very hazardous in a revolutionary ftate. The fame idea is recognized in all the American conftitutions : but they were not form-ed whilft the independence of the country was at hazard. The printers in favour of the claims of Great-Britain, had, in the time of the revolution-ary war, no ftanding in united America, excepting within the lines of the Britifh army. Our com-mittes of correfpondence, our county, and colo-nial conventions, were the authors of the domo-ciliary vifits, and took care of the unfriendly printers and writers, until our governments were formed : and then, laws duly made, prohibited, under the moft fevere penalties, the writing, printing, or fpeaking, any thing againft the inde-pendence of the United States, or in favour of the claims of the Britifh King upon the American colonies.

Had this been omitted, our country would have teemed with preffes devoted to the Britifh crown, and with artful mercenary writers, even native Americans, to diftract our counfels, and to divide and difunite our people.

J. I.   REVIEW

Capitol! This historic volume is a folio bound in half sheep. Its title is 'An Account of the Receipts and Expenditures of the United States, For the Year 1810. Stated in pursuance of the standing order of the House of Representatives of the United States, passed on the thirtieth day of December, one thousand seven hundred and ninety-one. Washington: A. & G. Way, Printers. 1812.'

Its historical rescue from the burning Capitol is briefly recorded by the Admiral himself, who has written inside the volume, 'Taken in the President's room in the Capitol, at the destruction of that building by the British, on the capture of Washington 24th August 1814 by Admiral Cockburn and by him presented to his eldest brother Sir James Cockburn of Langton, Bart, Governor of Bermuda.'

The volume is entirely undamaged by fire, and its green morocco label, lettered in gold on the front cover 'President of the United States,' is intact.

Jefferson was as indignant as anyone at the terrible loss caused by the fire and decided to sell his great library to the National Government at far less than its value. He wrote to Congressman Samuel H. Smith the following letter:

You know my collection, its condition and extent. I have been fifty years making it, and have spared no pains, opportunity or expense, to make it what it is. While residing in Paris, I devoted every afternoon I was disengaged, for a summer or two, in examining all the principal bookstores, turning over every book with my own hand, and putting by everything which sufficiently advanced to enable him to make it his permanent home. He was from home when the fire took place at Shadwell, and the first inquiry he made of the Negro who carried him the news was after his books. 'Oh, my young master,' he replied carelessly, 'they were all burnt; but, ah! we saved your fiddle.' Curiously enough, it was on account of another fire that his splendid collection is now safely, we hope, preserved in the Library of Congress.

On July 22, 1814, the joint naval and military forces of the British under Admiral Sir George Cockburn and Major-General Ross entered Washington, and set fire to many of the state buildings, including the Capitol, which then housed the Library of Congress. The loss of books and records was irreparable.

Indignation was expressed by everyone. Not since the burning of the Alexandrian Library by the Mahometans, it was said, had such a deed been perpetrated. Even the English newspapers were unanimous in their condemnation; a Nottingham journal stated that it was 'an act without precedent in modern wars or in any other wars since the inroads of the Barbarians who conflagrated Rome and overthrew the Roman Empire.'

Both General Ross and Admiral Cockburn lamented the destruction of the library. 'Had I known it in time,' said the former, 'the books most certainly would have been saved.' The Admiral gave practical proof of his sense of the loss, for a short time ago I was fortunate enough to secure a book which he himself rescued with his own hands from the burning

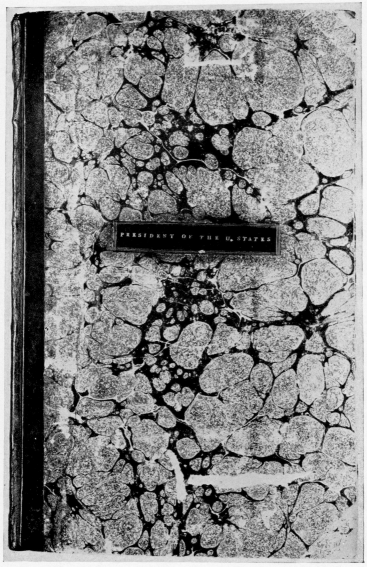

VOLUME RESCUED FROM THE CAPITOL WHEN IT WAS BURNT
BY THE BRITISH, 1814

related to America, and, indeed, whatever is rare
and valuable in every science. Besides this, I had
standing orders during the whole time I was in
Europe on its principal book-marts, particularly
Amsterdam, Frankfort, Madrid, and London, for
such works relating to America as could not be found
in Paris. So that in that department particularly
such a collection was made as probably can never
again be effected, because it is hardly probable that
the same opportunities, the same time, industry, per-
severance, and expense, with some knowledge of the
bibliography of the subject, would again happen to
be in concurrence. During the same period, and after
my return to America, I was led to procure, also,
whatever related to the duties of those in the high
concerns of the nation, so that the collection, which I
suppose is of between nine and ten thousand volumes,
while it includes what is chiefly valuable in science and
literature generally extends more particularly to the
American Statesman.

Of course, when the project of the sale of Jefferson's
library to the Government was first broached, it
created a great uproar. The Washington correspond-
ent of the *Boston Gazette* wrote, 'The grand library of
Mr. Jefferson will undoubtedly be purchased with all
its finery and philosophical nonsense.' Some of the
members of Congress regarded the books as 'immoral,
indecent, irreligious, and generally revolutionary.'
Congressmen would!!! However, the measure passed
and the Government secured, for the sum of $23,950,
Jefferson's library, probably one quarter of what it
was worth even at that time. It consisted, when
purchased by the Library of Congress, of about seven

thousand volumes and was without doubt the best-chosen collection of its size in this country. The library was removed from Monticello to Washington in May, 1815, and a catalogue was printed in that year, which in its one hundred and seventy pages comprised exclusively the books purchased from Jefferson.

From the time of the sale until his death, Jefferson continued the collecting of books. This second library, consisting of about a thousand volumes, he bequeathed to the University of Virginia, but since the condition of his estate required that the library be disposed of to pay debts, it was sold at auction in Washington, February 27, 1829, by Nathaniel P. Poor, with a printed catalogue of nine hundred and thirty-one items. Thus many books with his autograph were scattered through the country. Incidentally the Library of Congress bought a few important volumes and manuscripts at this sale.

It was the irony of fate that in another disastrous fire which burned the Library of Congress, December 24, 1851, about two thirds of the original Jefferson collection, including the newspapers, was destroyed.

Jefferson never possessed a bookplate. Only occasionally he wrote his name on the title-pages of volumes, and because of the sale in 1829, some of these turn up for sale. The American Antiquarian Society only recently obtained a bound volume of the early pamphlet reports of its own organization, of which Jefferson was elected a member in 1814. On the first text leaf of the first pamphlet are his initials and at the top of the first page of the last pamphlet is his autograph. He had a secret and ingenious way of marking his books. Before the signature letter 'J,' or interchangeably 'I,' he wrote in a microscopic hand his own first initial, 'T.' After the signature letter 'T,' if there were that many signatures in the book, he wrote the letter 'J,' thus having his own initials 'T. J.' hidden in each volume. The books now remaining in the Library of Congress are thus marked. In the *New York Evening Post* of October 22, 1898, Ainsworth R. Spofford, Librarian of Congress, wrote a long article on 'Thomas Jefferson's Books,' which forms an excellent and authentic source of information.

The fourth, fifth, and sixth Presidents — Madison, Monroe, and John Quincy Adams — were all collectors of books. Their activities were mostly in the field of Americana, and all three were purchasers of pamphlets and tracts relating to the first settlements in their native States. They collected articles about themselves, and their activities while President. I do not think they were controlled unduly by vanity, but their careers were really interwoven with the formative period of this country. Thomas Jefferson was interested in the discovery of the western portion of this hemisphere and gathered all the material he could on this interesting subject. It was he who was the inspiration of Lewis and Clark in their great journey across the continent. Madison, Monroe, and Adams also followed in Jefferson's footsteps and collected books relating to this great enterprise.

Madison, especially after his retirement, was a great reader of books and was considered by literary men as their patron. His library, which consisted largely of books sent to him by numerous authors, occupied an ample room in his house at Montpelier. He never possessed a bookplate. A considerable number of his books were sold by Stan. V. Henkels, May 9, 1899, in the final settlement of the estate of Dolly Madison.

President Monroe, although not a scholar or a man of general culture, was especially interested in history. He must have had a fairly large library, judging from the manuscript numbers entered on his type-set book-label, of which there were two varieties of border. A portion of his private library was sold at auction by W. M. Morrison, auctioneer, at Washington on February 24, 1849.

John Quincy Adams was much given to reading, especially in history and poetry, and possessed a large library. This collection is now housed in a stone building next to the John Quincy Adams home in Quincy, Massachusetts, and is owned by the Adams Memorial Society, formed in 1927 to take over the Adams house and to keep it open for the use of the family as a memorial to their ancestor. The library consists of nearly ten thousand volumes, although about a tenth of these were added by the two following generations. In 1933, the most valuable of the volumes, about seven hundred and fifty in number, were deposited by the family in the Boston Athenaeum. John Quincy Adams had at least four different bookplates. The first was a crudely engraved label, with his name, and the copy in the

A

LETTER

From a VIRGINIAN,

TO THE

Members of the Congress

TO BE HELD

At PHILADELPHIA,

ON

The firft of SEPTEMBER, 1774.

PRINTED IN THE YEAR 1774.

American Antiquarian Society collection bears the date 1782 in his handwriting. The other three plates are heraldic, with the family arms, excellently engraved, but without name of engraver.

With John Quincy Adams ends the first fifty years of the Republic. He was the last President who came under the influence of eighteenth-century culture. The libraries of the first six Presidents all contained volumes of Chesterfield, Goldsmith, Sterne, Doctor Johnson, and Voltaire. There were, of course, religious books in the presidential collections, but they are usually found, in the bookseller's parlance, in 'good unused condition.' Although 'Tom Jones' was in nearly all the libraries of the Presidents, I failed to find a single volume of Richardson's 'Pamela or Virtue Rewarded.' Perhaps they felt that election to the Presidency was sufficient reward and acknowledgment of their political chastity!

We have not the space to dwell at length on the Presidents between John Quincy Adams and Lincoln. Jackson, although not a man of culture, was a lover of literature and frequently read Shakespeare. He had a fairly extensive library at The Hermitage, although an inventory of his house made in 1825 showed only one bookcase in three sections. He had no bookplate, but often scribbled his signature on the title-pages of his books. The Hermitage was burned with all its contents in 1834. Jackson ordered it rebuilt and lived there until his death in 1845. A number of books from his library were sold at the American Art Association, April 13, 1927.

Van Buren's library, although large, consisted mostly of law-books, theology, and political economy. About eighteen years ago one of my present associates, Mr. Percy E. Lawler, who was then working for a New York firm of booksellers, was asked to go to Fishkill Landing on the Hudson to the old Verplanck homestead to look at the library of President Van Buren. He arrived on a raw February day and was shown into a bare, unheated room in which he was told the Order of the Cincinnati was inaugurated. At one end of this room were a large number of books in piles on the floor. They had previously been kept in a barn that was not entirely waterproof, for all, or the majority of them, were so rain-soaked that it was impossible to separate one leaf from another. The loss, however, was not so great, as they consisted of uninteresting volumes of theology which their proud authors had presented to the President. Van Buren had a small engraved bookplate. In the Association of the Bar of the City of New York is a collection of law-books from his library, with a bookplate stating that they were the gift of Silas B. Brownell in 1904. A number of books from his library were sold at the Walpole Galleries, July 31, 1923.

William Henry Harrison, descended from a distinguished Virginia family, had a small library, containing a number of good books either inherited or acquired. He died within a month after assuming the Presidency, and therefore had not the later lifetime granted to many Presidents for reading and leisure. He possessed no bookplate. John Tyler owned an extensive library and was well educated and well read — familiar with the classics, with Addison, Steele, Goldsmith, Johnson, and Byron, to whom he frequently referred in letters to his children. Much of his library was destroyed during the Civil War. In one of the volumes which descended to his son, Lyon G. Tyler, the latter wrote, 'This was one of the few books of his library preserved from the ravages of the Northern Troops at his residence, "Sherwood Forest," Charles City Co., Virginia.' President Tyler owned a small book-label, with the motto, 'Luxuria et egesta commodis cedunt,' which he probably acquired soon after his father's death in 1813.

The years from 1845 to 1861 were rather barren for presidential libraries, and Polk, Taylor, Fillmore, Pierce, and Buchanan are more interesting to the student of politics than to the literary historian. The lawyers among them gathered American law-books of the period, which take almost the lowest place in the mind of the collector. President Fillmore might be excepted from the above general statement. He possessed a library of about five thousand volumes and had two printed book-labels, one for his 'Law Library' and one for his 'Miscellaneous Library.' In the Grosvenor Library Bulletin for September, 1920, is a lengthy account of Fillmore's library, based on a manuscript catalogue of the books drawn in the President's hand. The collection contained a great number of miscellaneous books on history, travels, education, and literature. Noteworthy are three books on wines, showing that the statesmen of that day were far from teetotalers. Shortly after Mr. Fillmore's death in 1874 his library was sold at auction. Some of his most interesting books appeared in the De Puy sale at Anderson's in 1925. It is recorded that when Fillmore took possession of the Executive Mansion, it contained no books, not even a Bible. Fillmore secured an appropriation from Congress for the purchase of books and fitted up as a library the largest and most cheerful room on the second story.

Franklin Pierce owned a fairly good library of standard literature, about two hundred volumes of which are now owned by his nieces at Hillsborough, New Hampshire, although some of the especially interesting volumes were selected by the New Hampshire Historical Society.

We come now to Abraham Lincoln. He was, as is well known to everyone, a great reader. I cannot state that he was a book-collector, but there is no doubt that he was a book-lover. His copy of Shakespeare was purchased by the late Henry Clay Folger and is now placed in his great library of Shakespeariana in Washington. Lincoln had no time in the four years and forty days in which he was President to devote himself to books, although the reading of his younger days was reflected in his every act. Probably no man that ever lived had a greater command over the English language than Abraham Lincoln. He studied the lexicon, and there is in existence today his own copy of Noah Webster's Dictionary for Primary Schools, published in New York in 1833. On the fly-

Springfield, Nov. 30 1858

H. C. Whitney, Esq

My dear Sir:

Being desirous of preserving, in some permanent form, the late joint discussion between Douglas and myself, ten days ago I wrote to Dr. Ray, requesting him to forward to me, by express, two sets of the Nos. of the Tribune, which contain the reports of those discussions— Up to date I have no word from him on this subject— Will you, if in your power, procure them and forward them to me by Express? If you will, I will pay all charges, and be greatly obliged to boot—
Hoping to meet you before long I remain

As ever Your friend
A. Lincoln

LINCOLN'S LETTER CONCERNING HIS FAMOUS DEBATE WITH
DOUGLAS

leaf is written, 'A. Lincoln, Esq. Attorney and Counsellor at Law, Springfield, Ill.' and on the title-page is the autograph, 'A. Lincoln, Springfield, Ill. Sangamon County.'

Lincoln had many books of sterling quality, such as Gibbon's 'Decline and Fall of the Roman Empire,' Hallam's 'View of the State of Europe during the Middle Ages,' and other books of history, poetry, and philosophy. In 1860, Lincoln was elected the sixteenth President of the United States. He knew that troublesome times were upon him. He gave to his law partner, William H. Herndon, a large part of his literary library just before his departure for Washington to take up his presidential duties. Lincoln had many law-books which would be worthless were it not for the magic name, 'A. Lincoln,' written on the title-page. His own copy of the first edition of his debates with Stephen A. Douglas, published in Columbus in 1860, was in the famous Lambert collection. Lincoln gave it to a friend and it bears the following autograph inscription on the fly-leaf: 'A. Lincoln to W. M. Cowgill.' Inserted in this copy are two autograph letters of Lincoln's in one of which he modestly states that 'Being desirous of preserving in some permanent form the late joint discussion between Douglas and myself, ten days ago I wrote to Dr. Ray, requesting him to forward to me, by express, two sets of the Nos. of the Tribune, which contain the reports of those discussions — Up to date I have no word from him on the subject — Will you, if in your power, procure them and forward them to me by Express? If you will, I will pay all charges, and be greatly obliged to boot.'

In the Mitchell autograph sale held at Henkels, December 5, 1894, were included twelve titles, in twenty-two volumes, from the law library of Lincoln & Herndon, with the firm name entered in each volume.

Of the immediate successors to Lincoln, Andrew Johnson had few books, but President Hayes had a large library of over eight thousand volumes, about half of which was Americana and Western items, including the collection of Robert Clarke, the Cincinnati dealer and collector. This library was removed in 1916 from the Hayes homestead to the Hayes Memorial at Fremont, Ohio. Mr. Hayes had no personal bookplate. He personally collected all his books and frequently bid for them at auction. The following letter to W. O. Davie and Company, the well-known booksellers of Cincinnati, Ohio, has only recently come into my hands.

Fremont, O.
26 Dec. 73.

Gentlemen:

I will give for books to be sold on the first as follows viz

No. 18 Lincoln by Gannon	3.50
" 63 Franklin by Bigelow	3.30
" 65 Garden Management	2.75
" 157 Cornelius Cook book interlined	1.65

Sincerely

R. B. HAYES

W. O. DAVIE & Co.
16 E. 4th Cin. O.

army.

Fremont, O.
26 Dec, 73

Gentlemen:

    I will give for books to be sold on the first as follows viz

No 18 Lincoln by Lamon   3.50
" 63 Franklin by Bigelow   3.30
" 65 Garden Management   2.75
" 157 Cornelius Cook book in <u>trimmed</u> 1.65

                  Sincerely
                  R B Hayes

W O Davie & Co
16 E 4th Cin. O

PRESIDENT HAYES ORDERS SOME BOOKS

It is not generally known that Grant was interested in good books. When a student at West Point, hardly twenty-one years old, he wrote as follows:

U. S. Military Academy West Point
March 8, '43

Messrs. Carey & Hart

Sirs

Within enclosed you will find $2.00. the cost of the illustrated editions of 'Charles O'Malley' and 'Harry Lorrequer.' These works will be sent to my address at this Post Office.

Yours &

CADET U. S. GRANT

General Grant's rather large library descended to his son, Ulysses S. Grant, Jr. The son spent his last days in San Diego, California, and his father's library was for a long time in glass-door bookcases on the mezzanine of the U. S. Grant Hotel. When Doctor Edgar Hewitt was organizing the San Diego Museum from material left by exhibitors at the 1915 Exposition, he secured the Grant library as a gift, and it is now in the beautiful California Building in Balboa Park. The library contains about twelve hundred volumes broadly selected, chiefly in the fields of history — ranging from Herodotus to Macaulay — and literature, including the American and English classics. There is also a set of Audubon's 'Birds and Quadrupeds,' and the Bible upon which the President took the oath of office. The reason for the excellent selection was due to the group of Bostonians, who, learning that the White House has no adequate library, raised a fund to purchase such a collection, and inserted in each book a bookplate with the wording: 'Lieut. Gen. U. S. Grant, from Citizens of Boston, January 1, 1866.'

President Garfield, highly educated and a college president at twenty-six, possessed a library of about twenty-five hundred volumes, comprising the classics, modern literature, history, political science, and economics, with many books containing his marginal notes. This library is still at his home, 'Lawnfield,' Mentor, Ohio. His bookplate, with the motto, 'Inter Folia Fructus,' was a printed label, and has at least three slight variations. President Arthur, an honor student at college and possessing literary taste and culture, possessed a large library, principally strong in literature, biography, and economics. His books descended chiefly to his son, Chester Alan Arthur, now of Colorado Springs, Colorado. His bookplate was the Arthur crest, with the motto, 'Impelle Obstantia.'

Grover Cleveland was also a reader of good books. He owned quite a respectable library of about two thousand books. He did not have a bookplate but his wife had. The design portrays a woman writing on a scroll with a view of the Capitol and the arms of the United States. The lettering reads, 'Ex-libris Frances Folsom Cleveland.' President Cleveland was not much of a reader in the later years of his life, but when a young man at Buffalo read eagerly the current literature and biography of the period. His library, as it remained at his death, is still in the house at Princeton.

U.S. Military Academy, West Point March 31st [18]45

Messrs Carey & Hart

Sirs

Within inclosed you will find $2.00, the cost of the illustrated editions of "Charles O'Malley" and "Harry Lorrequer." These works will be sent to my address at this Post Office.

Yours &c

Cadet U. H. Grant

To Messrs Carey & Hart

GRANT WHEN A CADET ORDERS TWO BOOKS BY
CHARLES LEVER

Benjamin Harrison had a good library, chiefly of books which he wished to read or use — literature, history, biography, and reference books, most of which are in Mrs. Harrison's house at Indianapolis. Like other recent Presidents, he often sought relaxation in mystery stories. He continued in the practice of law after the Presidency and accumulated many law-books, some of which went to his son, Russell, and some to his daughter, Mrs. James Blaine Walker, Jr. President Harrison never owned a bookplate, according to his widow. An armorial plate of a Benjamin Harrison is of another family.

President McKinley had a modest library at his home in Canton, Ohio. Upon the death of Mrs. McKinley, it was divided among the heirs, each picking out what appealed to him. It contained four or five hundred volumes, the greater portion devoted to historical or economic subjects. The President and his brother, Abner McKinley, practiced law at Canton for a long number of years and jointly owned a law library. About 1890, Mr. Abner McKinley opened a law office in New York City and took the library with him. After his death in 1904, the law library was sold.

Theodore Roosevelt was a scholarly President. He was a great reader and a great collector. His study, gun-room, and trophy-room at Sagamore Hill all had books from the floor to the ceiling. He started to read early in life and often disapproved, according to Owen Wister, of the author's moral standpoint, especially when it did not agree with his own. Wister related the following:

Senior [Roosevelt] and sophomore [Wister] set small store upon most literature perfectly nice, well-behaved prose and verse, that read as if Alfred Tennyson or Charles Lamb had been diluted with warm water, and stirred round in a teacup by a teaspoon. But Roosevelt was not ready — never became ready — to go as far the Tom Jones way as I went, even in that day.

When Roosevelt became older, he started to collect books on subjects that interested him, particularly on birds and big-game hunting. Of the latter, we must refer to his autobiography.

Now, I am very proud of my big-game library. I suppose there must be many big-game libraries in Continental Europe, and possibly in England, more extensive than mine, but I have not happened to come across any such library in this country. Some of the originals go back to the sixteenth century, and there are copies or reproductions of the two or three most famous hunting books of the Middle Ages, such as the Duke of York's translation of 'Gaston Phoebus,' and the queer book of the Emperor Maximilian. It is only very occasionally that I meet any one who cares for any of these books. On the other hand, I expect to find many friends who will turn naturally to some of the old or the new books of poetry or romance or history to which we of the household habitually turn.

Roosevelt was proud of his reading and his acquaintance with rare and unusual books. He stated somewhere that he was in no sense a collector, which is very misleading, as he gives himself away when writing of his big-game library. He thought book collecting did not go with the wide-open spaces, or the other manly sports he so often mentions. Hunting after rare books has more thrills to the minute, in my estimation, than trapping wild animals in the jungle. The latter is child's play compared with it.

President Roosevelt might have accumulated a very large library through presentation copies alone. No president ever received so many gifts from writers and rulers all over the world. Also, when he was editor of the *Outlook* he wrote many reviews of books, which brought additional volumes to his library. His bookplate was really his father's plate, from which he struck off impressions from the original copper, since his father bore the same name and died when he was in college. The library today remains at Sagamore Hill, as part of the undistributed Roosevelt estate.

Speaking of President Roosevelt reminds me of old Bibles, for he was the only President of the United States, who, at his first induction into office, was not sworn on the Holy Scriptures. Most of the Presidents use the Bible at the inaugural and forget about it afterward. Roosevelt came to Buffalo when it was evident that McKinley would not survive the assassin's bullet. Everything had to be done hurriedly, and at the death of President McKinley, Mr. Roosevelt took the oath of office in the house of Mr. Ansley Wilcox, a prominent lawyer of Buffalo. The latter gentleman, in a letter dated October 15, 1903, writes:

> According to my best recollection, no Bible was used, but President Roosevelt was sworn with up-

lifted hand. There were Bibles, and some quite interesting ones, in the room and readily accessible, but no one had thought of it in advance, there being little opportunity to prepare for this ceremony, and when Judge Hazel advanced to administer the oath to the new President, he simply asked him to hold up his right hand, as is customary in this State.

The subject of Bibles of the Presidents is a fascinating one and I regret I cannot refer to it here. I cannot refrain from mentioning that Washington's Family Bible is in the Old Church in Alexandria, Virginia.

The beloved William Howard Taft was interested in books in a mild sort of way. No one was more painstaking and thorough than he in looking up original sources of information when forming an opinion, whether as President or Chief Justice. He liked to have books close to hand. He was interested enough in collecting to have his own bookplate. It is handsomely engraved and depicts his old homestead at Millbury, Massachusetts, with the scales of Justice and the arms of the United States. The books which he accumulated, rather miscellaneous in character, are mostly in his summer home at Murray Bay, Canada, although his law library is still located in his house at Washington.

Woodrow Wilson used books, but had no real love of them. He was like other university professors who use libraries but do not form them. Like all historians he had about him the apparatus of his profession, the works of reference and other books that would direct him in his studies. He liked up-to-date volumes, although he consulted original editions when writing his histories. He was a real adept at finding material, which is no mean praise. Woodrow Wilson used only one bookplate, which depicts a shelf of books, a facsimile of his signature, and the following quotation of his own making:

Council and Light
Knowledge with Vision
And Strength and Life and Pleasure withal.

Another plate was made for him, after his retirement from the Presidency, which consisted of a portrait of himself with the Church of Notre Dame in the background. According to Mrs. Wilson, he never used this plate in his books. His library is still intact in Washington.

Warren G. Harding, it is needless to state, was not a book-collector. I would like to claim him among the fraternity, but I regret I cannot. All his personal property including his library went to Mrs. Harding at the time of his death and she in turn gave the books to the Harding Memorial Association of Marion, Ohio.

Calvin Coolidge will probably go down in history as one of the wisest of the Presidents. He had the reputation of being extremely cautious, and I have a presentation copy of his 'Life,' by William Allen White, which seems to corroborate this statement. It bears on the fly-leaf in the President's writing: 'Without recourse. Calvin Coolidge.'

Mr. Coolidge was interested in the news of the world. He read of the sale in London of the original manuscript of 'Alice in Wonderland' which I had purchased. On my return from abroad in May, 1928, the President asked me to lunch at the White House and to bring with me the manuscript. I found that 'Alice in Wonderland' was one of his favorite books, that he was interested in Shakespeare, that he liked to own good editions. He asked me details of the first publication of 'Alice in Wonderland,' and I tried to explain to him that the first edition, issued in 1865, not being altogether to Carroll's liking, was suppressed. 'Suppressed?' said the President. 'I did not know there was anything off-color in Alice!'

Mr. Coolidge accumulated a large library when at the White House, from books presented to him and those acquired by himself. When he left Washington in 1929, forty cases of books, with over four thousand volumes, were sent to Northampton. Later, when the homestead at Plymouth was remodeled, place was made for these books and also some of the interesting books which he had read as a child and in his early life. When his friend, Frank W. Stearns, in 1926 sought to present him with a bookplate, Sidney L. Smith was commissioned to perform the task. He finally made a drawing with two panels, the lower showing the signing of the Mayflower Compact and the upper the homestead at Plymouth. But ill health intervened in 1928 and Mr. Smith was unable to cut the plate on copper, dying the following year. Timothy Cole was then engaged to engrave a plate on wood, which was finished in 1929, showing the Plymouth homestead, and above it, a bust of Washington.

COOLIDGE WAS CAUTIOUS WHEN HE GAVE AWAY BOOKS

Mr. Hoover is the greatest book-collector among the Presidents since Jefferson. He has an unusual faculty of delving in out-of-the-way places; in searching for material not readily accessible. He resembles Jefferson in that on all his journeys he gathered volumes that in time would be valuable to the student. Thus, when he was in China, in 1899, he gathered a most comprehensive collection of books, in many languages, on China and the Chinese people. This he gave to Stanford University, becoming the nucleus of the great Chinese library there. The Hoover War Library at Stanford is also a monument to his diligence and foresight as a collector. He gathered all through the war every document, pamphlet, proclamation, periodical, or broadside relating thereto, which in time will be the foundation material for the history of the great contest. This achievement is the greatest of any of the Presidents in the field of book-collecting.

In 1912, Herbert Clark Hoover and his wife, Lou Henry Hoover, issued in London a translation of Agricola's 'De Re Metallica,' from the first edition published in Basle in 1556. It is a treatise on mining and metals and is one of the classics of its kind. The notes by Mr. Hoover show a large knowledge of the subject and an intimate acquaintance with the rare books of the period. In fact, there are twelve books printed before 1500 mentioned in the original edition of Agricola. Mr. Hoover succeeded in securing all twelve!

In 1930, Mr. Hoover signed the bill making the

Vollbehr collection of Incunabula the property of the Nation. Included in it was a splendid copy of the Gutenberg Bible, printed on vellum. This acquisition is one of the notable achievements of Mr. Hoover's administration. It has endeared him to book-lovers everywhere.

Mr. Hoover's bookplate is a reproduction of one of the woodcuts in a very early book on mining, 'Ein Nutzlich Bergbüchlin von Allen Metallen,' 1557, with an interesting border. Christopher Morley's article in the *Saturday Review of Literature* in 1932 gives a graphic description of Mr. Hoover as a book-collector.

Franklin Delano Roosevelt, thirty-second President of the United States, has been interested in the gathering of books and manuscripts ever since he was a student at Harvard College. His researches into the early history of the American Navy have been noteworthy. Mr. Roosevelt is an adept at discovering original sources and has succeeded in uncovering historical material hitherto unknown. 'Our First Frigates, Some Unpublished Facts about their Construction, by the Hon. Franklin D. Roosevelt, assistant secretary of the Navy,' was published in 1914, and the President in this little pamphlet shows his skill as an archivist. Mr. Roosevelt has gathered for his library many books on the maritime history of the United States. He has not only accumulated the rarer volumes on the subject, but to his collection he has added early views, ship-models, contemporary manuscripts and autographs. His bookplate is a small engraved plate, with an anchor and four stars.

The President, with his real flair for collecting, should devote some of his energies to gathering the precious memorials of our country's history, so that they can be available for the use of scholars forever. No one can do it better. There are thousands of printed books, documents, and autograph letters in private possession that should be secured for the Library of Congress or the new department of National Archives in Washington. It is a noble project, and it is to be hoped that the President will give his personal attention to a matter that must be as dear to him as it is to the entire American public.

No one should look upon a book from the libraries of George Washington, Thomas Jefferson, or Abraham Lincoln without a thrill. The volumes from the Presidents' libraries mean much more to the student than their title-pages indicate. To the biographer they are of inestimable value. It is a pity that the great institutions of the United States do not contain more books that at one time belonged to our Presidents, for it is possible to obtain volumes from the private libraries of all of them.

VII

OLD ALMANACS AND PROGNOSTICATIONS

MY BROTHER'S parrot, Josephine, is quite a weather prophet. When she squawks from the reception-room of my New York library where she lives, 'Get out, you!' rasping her gray tail feathers against the brass bars of her cage, it's fairly certain to rain. If she whistles her repertoire of chromatic scales, the sun will soon be shining. But if she continues to address some invisible presence, we are in for a steady downpour.

Josephine was rasping her feathers one rainy afternoon last March when the doorbell rang. I was busy looking over my copy of Conrad's 'Lord Jim,' the perfect book to read on a rainy day. The stranger who came into my library introduced himself by saying that he had wanted to call on me for ages. He had some things he believed would interest me. Now, everyone with something to sell says that. Commonly the caller produces an old Bible, or a faded copy of the *Ulster County Gazette* containing an announcement of the death of George Washington, which invariably turns out to be a worthless reprint. But as this fellow began to shed manila envelopes from his pockets, I grew curious; and when he spread

ONE OF THE WORLD'S GREAT COLLECTIONS OF RARITIES,
1320 WALNUT STREET, PHILADELPHIA

them neatly before me on the desk, I became interested indeed. Much to my surprise, they contained very rare seventeenth-century New England
almanacs. Here was a find! What would he want for
them? I wondered.

Observing my interest, my caller began to pace
nervously about the room. I was reminded of another
distinguished collector and old friend who is a little
gone on first editions and manuscripts of Robert
Burns. The head of a conservative corporation, I
have often wondered what his board of directors
would think could they see him celebrating a happy
purchase in my office with an abandoned Highland
fling and maybe a wee doch-an-doris. But my caller
was as sober as a judge. He pointed out to me some
old prophecy contained in one of these almanacs that
had miraculously come true. This whetted my appetite the more as an embarrassing pause followed.
He took up his precious pamphlets and returned them
to his pockets.

'Doctor,' he began nervously, 'you don't know
what this means. Coming here has been sort of a trial
for me. I've collected these almanacs for years. I've
been haunted day and night, lately, with the idea of
having to sell them. I had thought of offering them
to you, but, now I've made up my mind, I just can't
part with them. I'd starve first!' With that, he waved
and rushed out. I have always regretted that I did
not ask his name and address. Although I was disappointed in not securing his blessed old almanacs, I
recognized in him a true collector.

There are many millions of people in the world to-day who still rely implicitly on the forecasts of the future contained in their favorite almanacs. There are thousands of farmers in this country alone who plant their crops according to weather predictions made in last year's calendar. Generally printed in December for use the year following, they contain predictions of the state of the weather for the next three hundred and sixty-five days. Thus, when one of them states that there will be a howling nor'easter on November twenty-eighth next, many of the readers will believe and pin their faith on it. And not infrequently these predictions turn out to be true.

I am reminded of a story told of an eminent New England almanac maker who one day, while extremely occupied with affairs of his press, was interrupted by his young printer's devil.

'Mr. Thomas, you've left out the prediction for July thirteenth,' he complained. 'What'll I put?'

'Tarnation, young man, can't you see I'm busy? Put what you please, but get out!' When the almanac came out, these startling words appeared opposite July 13: 'Rain, hail, and snow.' You can imagine the old fellow's language when he saw that. But on July thirteenth, according to records, it actually did rain, hail, and snow! The next year this almanac outsold all its competitors.

Forecasts have always existed, and will continue, I suppose, as long as the human race craves information concerning the future. Self-appointed prophets announce the end of the world with monotonous regularity. If someone says that the final cataclysm will occur next June first, at 4 A.M., there are always people gullible enough to believe the prediction.

Mother Shipton, the famous prophetess of Henry VIII's time, who lived near the Dropping Well, in the town of Knaresborough, was forever foretelling unhappy events. Reputed to have been sired by the Devil — her mother was regarded as a witch — Mother Shipton made so much of her unique reputation that her slightest utterance was considered seriously. Men shook in their shoes and women 'shivered in their shifts' when she began to describe the future. Yet such fantastic statements of things to come — flying boats, for instance, and ships that would sail under the sea — were, you must admit, rather good guesses. When she died, about 1561, her prophecies were already circulated the length and breadth of England. Mother Shipton also predicted the end of the world, saying it would occur in 1881, some three centuries after her own death. When that year arrived, it actually 'caused most poignant alarm in rural England, the people deserting their houses and spending the night in prayer in fields and churches and chapels.'

When I was a very small boy, I remember being one day with my uncle, Moses Polock, in his bookshop in Commerce Street, Philadelphia. Suddenly, an elderly woman — she was probably all of thirty — came running up the narrow stairs leading to the shop, to ask breathlessly for an old almanac. She wanted to know, she said, the exact date for the ending of the world as predicted by Mother Shipton. I recall that I felt quite frightened at her words, but was quickly consoled when my uncle replied, with a twinkle in his eye, 'Next year.'

I have followed many strange paths in my eagerness to assemble the world's great literary treasures, and I've succumbed at various times to various passions in the collecting game — the first Bibles, early juvenile books, Shakespeare quartos, rare Bunyans, letters of George Washington and Abraham Lincoln. They have been child's play as compared with trying to form a collection of old almanacs. These pamphlets are scarcer than the proverbial hen's teeth, and when one does pop up from some unexpected source, it is generally about to crumble away, having been held in so many eager hands over the centuries. Many of the printed ones survive only in a single copy. As for finding manuscript almanacs in use before the invention of printing, to do that is a miracle. There are perhaps a dozen in all the world, the property of museums and public libraries. I knew of exactly one in a private collection. A little calendar two inches wide and ten long, made in England in 1367. It is older than any example owned by the British Museum. Each of its ten vellum sheets is exquisitely illuminated with capital letters and miniatures. It was probably the property of some great châtelaine, who wore it hanging from her girdle, companion to a large bunch of keys. This copy, now in my possession, is attached to the original piece of brocaded material which undoubtedly circled a generous waist. When I

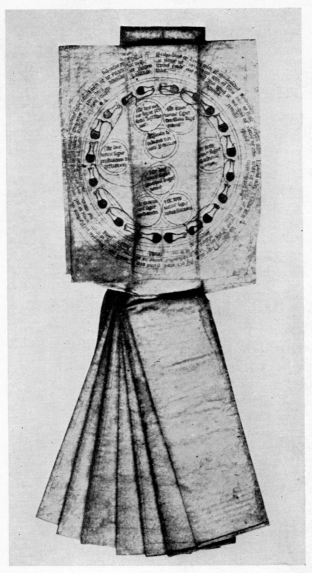

A MANUSCRIPT ALMANAC MADE IN ENGLAND IN 1367

first became aware of this almanac, it was owned by one of the greatest and most inspiring book-collectors of this country, the late William Augustus White. I often tried to pry it from him, but he, too, cherished it. One day about ten years ago, he came unexpectedly into my New York library, and, with an ingratiating smile, said, 'Doctor, I've come to the conclusion I cannot resist your importunities. This calendar really belongs in your collection.' Small as it is, amongst other things this little almanac contains a table of directions for calculating the leap year for one hundred and forty years. Speaking of leap years, perhaps it never belonged to a woman after all, but to some crusty old bachelor not unlike its present owner.

When Columbus set out on his voyage to discover a new passage to the Indies and only succeeded in discovering America, he used as his guide, the famous 'Perpetual Almanac' of the Spanish Jew, Abraham Zacuto. It was found among the papers of Columbus by his son, Ferdinand Columbus, who issued a life of the great explorer in 1571. There are no annotations in it, but the astronomical data correspond exactly with the calculations of Columbus, who was an expert in the science of navigation. It is now in the Colombina Library at Seville. A short time ago, Ernest Zinner, a professor of astronomy at Erlangen University, announced his discovery of an almanac issued at Königsberg in 1481, by Johann Müller. Professor Zinner believes that the notes in the margins are in the handwriting of Columbus, but I think it will turn out to be a dud. I have a copy of Zacuto's 'Almanach Perpetuum' for 1500, but alas! there are no annotations by Columbus.

For hundreds of years there existed a superstition that the gift of foretelling the future ran in certain families. Many almanacs were published by father and son, grandson, and so on, for generations. When a renowned almanac maker died without issue, someone was secretly selected to use his name and continue this profitable tradition. One of the most celebrated families of prognosticators began with John Laet in the sixteenth century. The Elizabethan poet, Sir Thomas Overbury, described an almanac maker as the worst part of an astronomer. The Laets were all astronomers and became renowned for the reliability of their prognostications. John Laet was succeeded by his son, Jasper Laet; next came Jasper Laet the younger, with Alphonsus, his brother, who wrote 'great and true prognostications' which were printed again and again in the sixteenth century. Some members of this family were also doctors of physic. Too bad they weren't veterinarians as well, as the cat was considered the best weather prophet of all. In a day when there were no barometers, the feline pet was looked to with a good deal of concern, watched as closely as an old sea captain observes his weather glass. Here is an ancient saying which was never known to fail:

> If cats do lick the forefeet and with them wash the head, it is a sign of rain.

Certain verses, better known than any in the Bible or Shakespeare, are in almost every almanac. There are people in the world who have never heard of Shakespeare, yet they know by heart these lines:

> Thirty days hath September,
> April, June and November,
> All the rest have thirty-one
> Save February which hath twenty-eight.

Until the beginning of the seventeenth century, the words ran as follows:

> Thirtie dayes hath November,
> Aprill, June and September,
> Februarie hath XXVIII alone,
> And all the rest have thirty and one.

As a rule, the following exception was added:

> But when of Leape Yeare commeth the time,
> Then dayes hath February twentie and nine.

In the late fifteenth and early sixteenth centuries, prognosticators and almanac makers were so confident of their powers of calculation that they composed their predictions to fit over a long period of time, generally from twelve to fifteen years. A few, more ambitious in their calculations, produced perpetual almanacs. This was bad business. They could sell a perpetual only once to a customer, while the later annual was certain of selling every year.

I am the happy owner of an amusing perpetual almanac, compiled by Leonard Digges, the famous English mathematician. The only other copy of this rare 1596 issue is in the British Museum. Read a

single page of 'A Prognostication everlasting,' and
if you can remember on what day of the week the
New Year began, you will know exactly what to expect. Here it is:

It is affirmed of some, when New yeares day falleth
on the Sunday, then a pleasant Winter doth ensue:
a naturall Summer: fruite sufficient: Harvest indifferent, yet some winde and raine: many mariages:
plentie of wine and honey: death of young men, and
cattell: robberies in most places: newes of Prelates,
of Kings: and cruell warres in the end.

On Monday, a Winter somewhat uncomfortable:
Summer temperate: no plentie of fruite: many fan-
sies and fables opened: agues shall raigne: Kings and
many others shall dye: Mariages shall be in most
places: and a common fall of Gentlemen.

On Tuesday, a stormie Winter: a wet Summer: a
divers Harvest: corn and fruite indifferent, yet
hearbes in gardens shall not flourish: great sicknesse of
men, women, and young children. Beasts shall hun-
gerstarve, and dye of the batch: many shippes, galleis
and Hulkes shall be lost and the bloodie Fli-es shall
kill many men: all things deare, save corne.

On Wednesday, Lo a warme winter: In the ende
Snow and frost: a clowdie Summer, plentie of fruite,
of Corne, Hay, Wine and Honey: great paine to
women with childe, and death to infants: good for
sheep: newes of kings: great warres, battell and
slaughter toward the middest!

On Thursday, Winter and Summer windie: a rainie
Harvest: therefore wee shall have overflowings.
Much fruite: plentie of honey: yet flesh shall be
deare: cattell in generall shall dye: great trouble,
warres, etc. licencious life of the feminine sexe.

On Friday, Winter stormie: Summer scant pleas-

A mery pnosticacion

For the yere of Chrystes incarnacyon
A thousande fyue hundreth fortye & foure
This to pronoũcate I may be bolde
That whã the newe yere is come gone is ye olde.

A MERRY PROGNOSTICATION FOR 1544

ant: Harvest indifferent, little store of fruite, of wine and honey, corne deare: many bleare eyes: youth shall dye: Earthquakes are perceived in many places: plenty of thunders, lightnings, and tempests: with a sudden death of cattell.

On Saturday, a meane Winter: Summer very hot: a late Harvest: good cheape garden hearbs: much burning: plenty of Hempe, Flaxe and honey. Olde folke shall dye in most places: Fevers and Tercians shall grieve many people: great muttering of warres: murthers shall be suddenly committed in many places for slight matters.

Not everyone believed in the man with 'such a prognosticating nose,' as Beaumont and Fletcher characterize the almanac maker of their day. Common sense told some men that it was better to take medicine when ill than to wait until the moon should reach a certain sign of the zodiac. In 1544, a three-leaved pamphlet appeared anonymously in London, called 'A Mery Prognosticacion.' It is one of the earliest attempts to ridicule predictions. The author begins by thumbing his nose in verse:

> For the yere of Chrystes incarnacyon
> A thousande fyve hundreth fortye & foure
> This to pronostycate I may be bolde
> That whā the newe yere is come, gone is ye olde.

I purchased the only known copy of this quaint example of early satire, in the Britwell sale at Sotheby's March, 1924. It can be seen today at the great Henry E. Huntington Library at San Marino, California.

In the American Colonies during the latter half of the seventeenth century and throughout the eighteenth, there were more almanacs published than all other books combined. Often a man's entire library consisted of a single almanac, which he carried with him in his pocket. New England had no newspapers in these early days, and the only way the settler could determine holidays, fairs, church meetings, and sittings of the courts was by consulting almanacs. These were frequently interleaved by their owners, who then used them as diaries and memorandum books, jotting down from day to day any event which interested them, or making a note of anything they wished to remember. These almanac diaries are invaluable and interesting today because they reveal to us, in their interleaved pages, a glimpse of the intimate life and actual happenings in the first American homes. Sometimes they are our only source of historical information. It is, for instance, from the manuscript note made against June fifteenth by the Reverend Samuel Haugh, of Reading, Massachusetts, in his almanac for 1648, that we learn of a very gruesome event, the first execution in New England for witchcraft.

The late Mr. George Brinley, of Hartford, Connecticut, who formed one of the greatest collections of Americana, was fortunate enough to secure this almanac, together with four others which had belonged to the Reverend Mr. Haugh, and had been annotated by him, all unique copies, printed between 1646 and 1653. A truly valuable source for the intimate history of our ancestors. The first one was a mere fragment, probably printed by Stephen Daye at his press in Cambridge, Massachusetts, the first in the Colonies. It is minus the title page and second and last leaves. The one dated 1647 came from the press of his son, Matthew Daye, and bears his imprint upon the title page.

From the middle of the seventeenth century on, the presses of New England were kept busy turning out almanacs. I believe there were hundreds of thousands of them issued before 1700. Yet strange to say, not more than three or four hundred are in existence today. The greatest collections belong to the Massachusetts Historical Society, the Library of Congress, the New York Public Library, and to the American Antiquarian Society in Worcester. My friend, Mr. Clarence S. Brigham, the director of the last-named institution, has for many years made a tireless search for early almanacs. Given the slightest clue, he is out, following the scent. As a result, he has unearthed many extraordinary examples.

Who were responsible for the material in these almanacs? Not 'spoiled' astronomers, but men of substance whose names counted for something more in colonial life than a doubtful ability to visualize the future. Samuel Danforth, one of the first graduates of Harvard College, was the author of early New England almanacs, and was succeeded by Israel and Nathaniel Chauncy, Nehemiah Hobart, John Foster, and William Brattle. Even Cotton Mather, that apostle of fire and brimstone, occasionally took time off from assuring his congregation of their certain damnation, to write almanacs. In 1687, John Tulley,

of Boston, began his famous series, issued every
year for fifteen years. He was the first American
author to begin the year with the month of January. His last almanac was called 'Tulley's Far-
wel, an Almanack for the year of Our Lord, 1702,
by John Tulley: who dyed as he was finishing this
Almanack; and so leaves it his Last Legacy to his
countrymen.'

In collecting these American almanacs I have been
very lucky. During my early years I dreamed of
some day finding first issues of two almanacs, the most
famous ones in American history. Each existed in a
single copy, but neither was a first issue. They were
safely locked up in the library of the Historical
Society of Pennsylvania, which I used to haunt as a
boy. These two almanacs had an uncanny fascina-
tion for me, and while hanging about the rooms I no
doubt made myself a nuisance to Mr. Frederick L.
Stone, then director of the society. He was more of a
collector than a librarian, and it was during his
custodianship, assisted by the great bibliographer,
Charles R. Hildeburn, that the society secured many
of its real treasures.

The first of these two little volumes, Atkins's
'Kalendarium Pennsilvaniense, or, America's Mes-
singer. Being an Almanack for the Year of Grace,
1686,' was the earliest production of a printing press
in the Middle Colonies, and the first work issued by
William Bradford, who had the distinction of printing,
not only the first book in Pennsylvania, but in New
York as well. Little is known of Samuel Atkins, but

Kalendarium Pennsilvaniense;

OR,

America's Meſſinger.

B.EING AN

ALMANACK

For the Year of Grace, 1686.

Wherein is contained both the Engliſh & Forreign
Account, the Motions of the Planets through the Signs, with
the Luminaries, Conjunctions, Aſpects, Eclipſes; the riſing,
ſouthing and ſetting of the Moon, with the time when ſhe
paſſeth by, or is with the moſt eminent fixed Stars : Sun riſing
and ſetting, and the time of High-Water at the City of *Phi-*
ladelphia, &c.
With Chronologies, and many other Notes, Rules,
and Tables, very fitting for every man to know & have ; all
which is accomodated to the Longitude of the Province of
Pennſilvania, and Latitude of 40 Degr. north, with a Table
of Houſes for the ſame, which may indifferently ſerve *New-*
England, New York, Eaſt & Weſt Jerſey, Maryland, and moſt
parts of *Virginia.*

By *SAMUEL ATKINS.*

Student in the Mathamaticks and Aſtrology.

And the Stars in their Courſes fought againſt Seſera, Jndg. 5. 29.

Printed and Sold by *William Bradford* at *Philadel-*
phia in *Pennſilvania,* 1685.

in his preface 'To the Reader' he explains his reason
for venturing to write this 'Ephemeris or Almanack.'
He says in part:

> I have journied in and through several places, not
> only in this Province, but likewise in Maryland, and
> else where, and the People generally complaining,
> that they scarcely knew how the Time passed, nor
> that they hardly knew the day of Rest, or Lords Day,
> when it was, for want of a Diary or Day Book....

Bradford's own statement is a milestone in the
history of printing:

> Hereby understand that after great Charge and
> Trouble, I have brought that great Art and Mystery
> of Printing into this part of America believing it may
> be of great service to you in several respects, hoping
> to find Encouragement, not only in this Almanack,
> but what else I shall enter upon for the use and serv-
> ice of the Inhabitants of these Parts. Some Irregu-
> larities, there be in this Diary, which I desire you to
> pass by this year; for being lately come hither, my
> Materials were Misplaced, and out of order....

Only two copies of this Atkins almanac were
known: the one which so fascinated me, and another
that had at one time belonged to the indefatigable
Mr. Brinley, and was purchased at his sale by the late
Ogden Goelet, for $555. To the surprise of all col-
lectors, a copy turned up at auction in 1917. I was
determined to have it. When it was knocked down to
me for $1950, I was very much elated and became
curious to learn about the other known copies. I
wrote to Ogden Goelet's son, Robert, who began to
investigate. He discovered that the copy purchased

by his father nearly forty years before was mysteriously missing from his bookcase. The one I had so
proudly secured proved to be the Goelet copy. Of
course I returned it to Mr. Goelet immediately. But
when in the year of grace, 1935, it was offered for sale
in the dispersal of the great Goelet collection, I had
the good fortune to buy it a second time. This time I
hope it sticks. But the story doesn't end here.
Recently, when leaving a New York auction room, a
friend stopped me and inquired about the little
almanac. What, he asked, was the printer's address?
A little shamefacedly, I replied that I didn't know —
an incredible admission for one collector to make to
another. I rushed back to my library and read,
'Printed and Sold by William Bradford at Philadelphia in Pennsilvania, 1685.' I couldn't wait to get to
Philadelphia, so I telephoned and held the wire im-
patiently until I learned that the copy on the shelves
of the Historical Society bore the following imprint:

> Printed and sold by William Bradford, sold also by
> the Author and H. Murrey in Philadelphia, and
> Philip Richards in New York, 1685.

For me it was a thrilling moment, for I realized that
the latter copy is the second issue, with the New
York name a later addition, and, unknowingly, I had
purchased the only copy known of the first publication in the middle colonies. It was as though a golden
needle, whose presence I had never suspected, had
fallen out of a haystack into my surprised hands.

Atkins's 'Pennsylvania Almanac' was succeeded by

To the Reader.

IT hou be good to live vertuously, then, Epistle, thou goes not to understand the cause why I do endeavour, I do publish this Ephemeris or Almanack, which is many things; I having travailed in and through these several places, not only in this Province, but likewise in Maryland, and else where, and the People generally complained, that they scarcely knew how the Time of the year, nor that they could know the day of Poll, or Lords Day, when it was, for want of a Diary, or Day-Book, which we call an Almanack. And on the other side, the many my Travels met with ingenious Persons, that have been knowing of the Mathematical Arts, some of which have wanted in Followers to make use of their like therein; Like wise many a Severe Complaint from such as have wanted of Inhabitants, which are here. I was easily moulded, and did delight among us; but small Knowledge exercised, to pleasure those, my Country men with that which they wanted, although it be not compleated in that I wished, which I did prond in second &c. Resolved? I have reduced the Sun and Moon places, according to their mean Motion, to this Meridian, which is five hours Weg from the City of London: For the other Planets, I have taken them by whole Degrees, from the Ephemerides of that ingenious and Skilful Artist, Mr. John Gadbury, from whence the Fundamental is derived: The Lunar Aspects I have reduced to the Four that they happen here, as before. As to the Moon's rising and setting, I have used the Method of Mr. Vincent Wing formerly in his Almanack; that is, the Moons rising from Pole to Pole, and her setting from New to Pull, according to her ten place in the Ecliptick; for what profiteth to shew you the time of her rising and setting in the day figure, when is cannot be in. In beginning, I have somewhat given it, by Latitude and accordingly I have Signed THERETO to that Knowledge that I have made of it here, to my Moon of Signs, by the fixed stars, &c. I have (as easy) shown it all that when they may be best disposed,

discerned, Besides the Table of Houses, Table of Kings, &c. I had thoughts to have inserted a Figure of th' Moons Eclip, a small Draught of the form of this City and a Tablet to find the hour of the day by the Shadow of a Staff; but well accept you Tool go cause them in that form, that I would have them, nor time to calculate the other, for it is for this year, and was one promise it in the next, but likewise I need other more particular Notes and Observations, which shall not only be useful to this Province, but likewise to the neighbouring Provinces on both sides. In the mean time, except this my Mite, being my first Fruits, and you will encourage me, according to my Ability, to force you in what I may, or can, which I am

Philadelphia, the 3d. of the   } Samuel Atkins.
10th Month, December)
Anno 1685,

The Printer to the Readers.

HEre is underplaced this after great Charge and Trouble, I have brought thee great Art and Mystery of Printing into this part of America, believing it may be of service (more to you Several effects, hoping to find Encouragement, have enjoyed my Almanack, but what else I shall never upon for the use and service of the Inhabitants of these Parts. Some In advertise, those here in this Diary, which I desire you to pass by, whisper, for being so irksome, hither, my Materials were MISplaced, and out of order, whereupon I was forced to use figures of Letters of several Forts, but understanding the nature of making of this nature, and being importuned therein I ventured to make public this, Desiring you to accustomed as I shall by the next, (as I find myself disposed) to appear here a things compleater. And for the relief Cu... &c. Apprehend from their Bills, Books, Lett... very In venture, Warrants &c. and what else is wanting at Mulberry his force given and pro...d,

Publish... the 28th   W. Bradford.
lot...

those of the mighty Daniel Leeds, who came to
America before William Penn. In 1687 he wrote an
almanac printed upon a broadsheet, divided into
twelve parts, one for each month. The following year
he issued another in which he added some light,
foolish, and unsavory paragraphs which gave great
uneasiness to Friends. Later Leeds apologized to
the Friends at the Philadelphia Meeting. He ad-
mitted that in the almanac 'there are some particulars that are too light and airy for one that is a
Christian indeed.' He ended his apology modestly,
thus: 'This much from me, who am your friend, whilst
I am my own. Daniel Leeds, Burlington 8th of 12th
mo. 1687.' It is a pity that no copy of this almanac
survives. As it was no doubt suppressed by the
Quakers, we can imagine the worst.

All almanac makers, including our own Benjamin
Franklin, were notorious plagiarists, and Daniel
Leeds was no exception. Jacob Taylor, a rival, wrote
of Leeds in 1706, 'that unparalleled Plagiary and un-
reasonable Transcriber, D. Leeds who hath now for
19 years with a very large stock of Impudence,
filched matter out of other men's works, to furnish his
spurious Almanacs.' Daniel was succeeded by his
two praiseworthy sons, Titan and Felix Leeds, who
carried out the noble tradition, pilfering the words
and wisdom of other men. But more of Titan anon.

The earliest known almanac printed in the great
city of New York was Bradford's issue for the year
1694, of which two imperfect copies exist. But the
earliest one by a New York author survives in a

single example. It was edited by John Clapp and published in 1697. Clapp kept a house of entertainment 'about two mile without the City of New York at the place called the Bowry, which was generally the bating place where Gentlemen take leave of their friends going so long a Journey as from New York to Boston, in a partying glass or two of generous Wine.'

No one would believe that I had in my possession for years two of the most valuable New York almanacs and never dreamed that I owned them. I had bought them, paid for them, and had carried them home, yet I had never heard of them or seen them. A riddle? Yes. Some ten years ago, while in England visiting the library of a distinguished collector, I had, when taking leave, stumbled against a folio volume that someone had carelessly left on the floor. It turned out to be one of the most valuable books in the world, a perfect copy of the 'First Laws of New York,' printed by William Bradford in 1694, with additional 'Laws' to 1699. It was in its original calf binding. I purchased it, brought it in triumph to America. One day, years later, the beloved Wilberforce Eames, the great authority on American printing and printers, saw it on my shelves and asked if I had ever examined the binding for printer's waste.

Now, some of the most astounding finds had been made in taking apart old bindings which have been padded with waste pages. I had the ancient cover dissected by an expert. Doctor Eames looked over the resultant material and found two hitherto unknown almanacs, John Clapp's for 1699 and Jacob

Taylor's for the same year, both printed by Bradford. He also discovered, *mirabile dictu*, the manuscript copy for the printer of a 'Broadside Sheet Almanack' for 1699.

The 'American Almanack' for 1717 contains these sage words:

> The Times are very bad, not Men, for they
> Are grown so bad it is a shame to say.
> But let this TRUTH drop from my harmless Penn,
> TIMES would be better had we better MEN.

The second American almanac which I coveted in the Pennsylvania Historical Society was Benjamin Franklin's famous 'Poor Richard's Almanac,' issued for the first time in 1733. Lightning, the saying goes, never strikes twice in the same place. That is, lightning has always given that impression. If this is true, then lightning must be an awful liar, for I had a similar experience with Franklin's almanac of 1733 as with Atkins's 'Pennsylvania Almanac' of 1685. The title page of the one belonging to the Historical Society of Pennsylvania read 'Third Impression.' Bibliographers never took much stock in these words, believing that Franklin had craftily printed them on what was really the first edition to make the public believe that 'Poor Richard' had rapidly galloped into three editions and was already a best seller. About two years ago, a gentleman appeared at my Philadelphia office, with a series of almanacs, including the 'Poor Richard' of 1733. It was not until after I purchased it that I realized that the two words 'Third Impression' were missing from the title page. It thus turns out to be the only one known of the first issue of the first 'Poor Richard's Almanac.'

It is not exactly news to state that the most famous almanacs in America — in fact, the best known in the entire world — were those issued by Franklin in Philadelphia between 1733 and 1766. Franklin took part in drawing up the Declaration of Independence, the Articles of Confederation, and the Constitution of the United States, but I think he was more proud of his almanacs than of his great historical achievements. They were quoted throughout the colonies, and translated into many languages. In England they were mentioned in the same breath with the works of Addison and Steele, and in France 'La science du Bonhomme Richard' was a topic of conversation in the great salons of that period. These 'Poor Richard' almanacs were better known abroad than any other example of American literature.

When Franklin arrived from Boston to take up his residence in the City of Brotherly Love, Titan Leeds, the son of old Daniel Leeds, was making almanacs for Andrew Bradford. Jacob Taylor was also making almanacs for Franklin's old master, Samuel Keimer. In 1728, Franklin, with his partner, Meredith, issued an almanac consisting of a single leaf. It was, to quote the *Pennsylvania Gazette*, 'done on a large sheet of demi-paper, after the London manner.' He issued another almanac, by John Jerman, in 1731. But the great adventure began in 1732, when, alone, he brought out his 'Poor Richard' almanac for the following year, by Richard Saunders. The imprint

Poor Richard, 1733.

AN
Almanack

For the Year of Chriſt

1733,

Being the Firſt after LEAP YEAR:

And makes ſince the Creation	Years
By the Account of the Eaſtern *Greeks*	7241
By the Latin Church, when ☉ ent. ♈	6932
By the Computation of *W.W.*	5742
By the *Roman* Chronology	5682
By the *Jewiſh* Rabbies	5494

Wherein is contained

The Lunations, Eclipſes, Judgment of the Weather, Spring Tides, Planets Motions & mutual Aſpeɛts, Sun and Moon's Riſing and Setting, Length of Days, Time of High Water, Fairs, Courts, and obſervable Days.

Fitted to the Latitude of Forty Degrees, and a Meridian of Five Hours Weſt from *London*, but may without ſenſible Error. ſerve all the adjacent Places, even from *Newfoundland* to *South-Carolina*.

By *RICHARD SAUNDERS*, Philom.

PHILADELPHIA:

Printed and ſold by *B. FRANKLIN*, at the New Printing-Office near the Market.

reads, 'Printed and sold by B. Franklin at the New Printing Office near the Market.'

It covered twenty-four pages, and was issued in two forms — plain, and interleaved, so that it could be used as a diary. For a long time Franklin's contemporaries had been publishing almanacs modeled after stale English ones, which proved unprofitable. Franklin realized that people were bored. It was up to him to get the public's attention in order to get their money. This first great American advertising genius decided to amaze as well as amuse. His advertisement for his initial almanac started off naïvely enough in his own newspaper, the *Pennsylvania Gazette*, with a description of routine contents, such as 'Planets motions and Aspects, Weather, etc., beside many pleasant and Witty Verses, Jests and Sayings, Author's Motive of Writing, Moon no Cuckhold, Bachelor's Folly, Game for Kisses, Katherine's Love, Conjugal Debate, and Breakfast in Bed, all for 3s. 6d. per Dozen.' (87½ cents.) A stick of dynamite was hidden herein. In addition to the rather trite contents, there was included a 'Prediction of the Death of his Friend, Mr. Titan Leeds.'

You can imagine the excitement caused by this advertisement. Every friend of Titan Leeds, Franklin's rival in the almanac field, rushed to the nearest bookseller to secure a copy. News of this small volume spread like wildfire. Its circulation was enormous. The early demise of Mr. Titan Leeds was the chief topic of conversation in the little city of Philadelphia. After reading Franklin's reasons for bringing out a new kind of almanac, these fatal words follow:

Indeed, this motive would have had force enough to have made me publish an Almanack many years since, had it not been overpowered by my regard for my good friend and fellow-student, Mr. Titan Leeds, whose interest I was extreamly unwilling to hurt. But this obstacle (I am far from speaking it with pleasure), is soon to be removed, since inexorable death, who was never known to respect merit, has already prepared the mortal dart, the fatal sister has already extended her destroying shears, and that ingenious man must soon be taken from us. He dies, by my calculation, made at his request, on Oct. 17, 1733, 3 ho., 29 m., P.M. By his own calculation he will survive till the 26th of the same month. This small difference between us we have disputed whenever we have met these nine years past; but at length he is inclinable to agree with my judgment. Which of us is most exact, a little time will now determine. As, therefore, these Provinces may not longer expect to see any of his performances after this year, I think myself free to take up the task, and request a share of publick encouragement, which I am the more apt to hope for on this account, that the buyer of my Almanack may consider himself not only as purchasing an useful utensil, but as performing an act of charity to his poor Friend and servant R. Saunders.

This statement caused a great sensation; the stick of dynamite went off with a bang. All his friends went to condole with Mr. Leeds, who was doubtless a little white about the gills. Almanac makers are as gullible as their patrons. Naturally, Mr. Leeds was quite anxious when October seventeenth dawned. In the meantime, Franklin's almanac was selling beyond his greatest hopes, and copies were distributed throughout the colonies. Titan comes back at Franklin in his 'American Almanac' for 1734, in which he mentions that notwithstanding Franklin's false prediction, 'I have by the Mercy of God lived to write a Diary for the Year 1734, and to publish the Folly and Ignorance of this presumptuous Author ... who proposes to succeed me in Writing of Almanacks.' He goes on to say that Franklin has usurped the place of the Almighty and manifested himself a fool and a liar. 'And by the mercy of God,' he writes, 'I have lived to survive this conceited Scriblers Day and Minute whereon he has predicted my Death; and as I have supplyed my Country with Almanacks for three seven Years by past, to general Satisfaction, so perhaps I may live to write when his Performances are Dead. This much from your annual Friend, Titan Leeds. October 18, 1733, 3 ho. 33 min. P.M.'

Franklin's retort courteous in the 'Poor Richard' for 1734 is a little masterpiece:

> In the preface to my last Almanack, I foretold the death of my dear old friend and fellow-student, the learned and ingenious Mr. Titan Leeds, which was to be the 17th of October, 1733, 3 h., 29 m., P.M. By his own calculation, he was to survive till the 26th of the same month, and expire in the time of the eclipse, near 11 o'clock, A.M. At which of these times he died, or whether he be really yet dead, I cannot at this present writing positively assure my readers; for as much as a disorder in my own family demanded my presence, and would not permit me, as I had intended, to

be with him in his last moments, to receive his last embrace, to close his eyes, and do the duty of a friend in performing the last offices to the departed. Therefore it is that I cannot positively affirm whether he be dead or not; for the stars only show to the skilful what will happen in the natural and universal chain of causes and effects; but 'tis well known, that the events which would otherwise certainly happen, at certain times, in the course of nature, are sometimes set aside or postpon'd, for wise and good reasons, by the immediate particular disposition of Providence; which particular dispositions the stars can by no means discover or foreshow. There is, however, (and I cannot speak it without sorrow,) the strongest probability that my dear friend is no more; for there appears in his name, as I am assured, an Almanack for the year 1734, in which I am treated in a very gross and unhandsome manner, in which I am called a false predicter, an ignorant, a conceited scribler, a fool, and a lyar. Mr. Leeds was too well bred to use any man so indecently and so scurrilously, and moreover his esteem and affection for me was extraordinary; so that it is to be feared that pamphlet may be only a contrivance of somebody or other, who hopes, perhaps, to sell two or three years' Almanacks still, by the sole force and virtue of Mr. Leeds' name. But, certainly, to put words into the mouth of a gentleman and a man of letters against his friend, which the meanest and most scandalous of the people might be ashamed to utter even in a drunken quarrel, is an unpardonable injury to his memory, and an imposition upon the publick.

Titan Leeds did not pass away until six years later. By that time Franklin had captured the entire almanac-reading public.

Of the almanacs issued from Franklin's press, beginning in 1733 and ending in 1766, no complete set exists. One of the best is that presented by the Curtis Publishing Company to the library of the University of Pennsylvania. Down to 1758 Franklin wrote every almanac himself, adding enough spice to each issue to insure a constant sale. In the 'Poor Richard' for 1758, which is in the Grolier Club's list of 'One Hundred Books Famous in English Literature,' Franklin collected from his previous almanacs all his famous sayings, which have since become household words. The following are among the 'familiar quotations':

> Here comes Glib-tongue, who can outflatter a Dedication; and lie, like ten Epitaphs.

> Mary's mouth costs her nothing, for she never opens it but at others' expense.

> He does not possess wealth, it possesses him.

> He that falls in love with himself will have no rivals.

> Onions can make ev'n heirs and widows weep.

> Lost Time is never found again.

> Little strokes fell great Oaks.

> Three removes are as bad as a Fire.

> Fools make feasts and wise men eat them.

> What is a Butterfly? At best He's but a Caterpillar drest.

And how about this familiar wail?

> Pray, Father Abraham, what think you of the Times? Wont these heavy taxes quite ruin the Country? How shall we ever be able to pay them?

The success of 'Poor Richard' naturally attracted many imitators, poor in fancy and 'poor' in name, such as Poor Will, Poor Ned, Poor Roger, Poor Thomas, Poor Job, and one, more audacious, Poor Richard Improved!

Christopher Sauer, of Germantown, Pennsylvania, printed almanacs in English and German. The story is told of a farmer threatening to sue him because of damage to his goods, owing to a false statement in one of his calendars. Arriving at the printing office soaking wet, when fine weather was predicted, he lambasted Sauer, asking him to reimburse him for his loss. 'Oh, friend,' the printer replied, 'friend, be not thus angry, for although it was I that made the almanac, the Lord God made the weather.'

In 1793, Robert B. Thomas began publishing, in Boston, the 'Old Farmer's Almanac,' now in its one hundred and forty-third year. Some newspapers still issue almanacs. Instead of a few pages, as of old, they now sometimes run to a thousand.

It is a pity the almanac-makers, with their gift of prophecy, could not foretell the depression. They would have saved us a lot of trouble. In the golden period before 1929, our friends in Wall Street usurped the place of the old almanac-makers. They told, for instance, that the P. D. Q. Railroad, then at 50, would sell at 500. They were exactly like the ancient prognosticators, but unfortunately for most of us, their predictions did not turn out so well.

The eternal twelve signs of the zodiac and the Moon's Man still decorate every almanac. Even to-

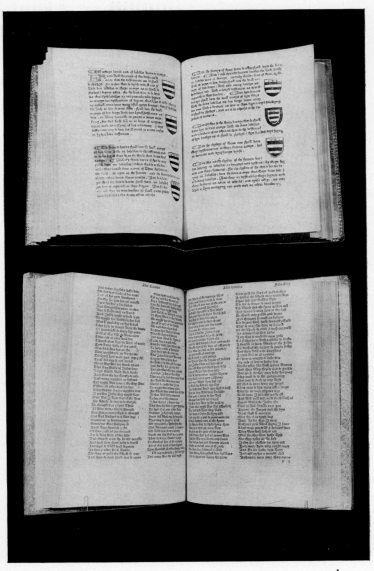

TWO GREAT BOOKS RARELY FOUND PERFECT: CAXTON'S
EDITION OF GOWER'S 'CONFESSIO AMANTIS' AND
JULIANA BERNER'S 'BOOK OF ST. ALBANS'

day the makers use the old familiar aphelion and perihelion, perigee and apogee, and the stereotyped signs representing the sun, moon, and earth. They contain also those ancient symbols, Aries, Gemini, Leo, Virgo, Scorpio, Sagittarius, and the other glorious reminders of the astrologers. To my mind, each almanac should have on its cover, Taurus — the Bull.

VIII

MUNCHAUSEN AND COMPANY

IT IS curious how few really great liars there have
been in the world. Mediocre and petty liars have
always existed, but the really great outstanding
first-class liars have been extraordinarily few. Possibly the awful fate of Ananias and Sapphira may
have had its due effect upon posterity. There has
certainly always been found in every age and in
every clime a prejudice against the prevaricator:

> The Lord delights in them that speak
> The words of truth; but ev'ry liar
> Must have his portion in the lake
> That burns with brimstone and with fire.

So sang Doctor Watts, and it was not an encouraging
prospect for the followers of Ananias. No wonder
most of us prefer to tell the less imaginative but
much safer truth!

Some men are remembered for a single, dignified
lie, like the sea-captain, for instance, who swore upon
a stack of Bibles that he had seen the fabulous sea-
serpent. And Marco Polo. He honestly believed he
had seen the unicorn! Any small boy reading his
'Voyages' today would know that it was only a
rhinoceros. It is only of the liars that have reached
the pinnacle of immortality that I sing.

By lying, I do not mean triumphs of the imagination, as in Dante or Blake. The world has always been inspired and influenced by persons of magnificent vision. Blake described graphically the ghost of a flea. This was fantasy at its highest flight, but it can find no place in our mundane category.

Great lying is an achievement. A survey of the literature of all nations produces but few liars of really first-class rank. Strangely enough there is not a woman among them.

It is a difficult task collecting first editions of books containing the world's most magnificent lies. They are among the world's rarest books, for they were always very popular and consequently were literally read to tatters. It is almost impossible to secure them in good condition. Is there any greater proof of their excellence?

The first great liar of whom we have record was a Biblical gentleman who was apparently unafraid of hell fire. His one stupendous lie possibly changed the whole course of civilization. I refer to Jacob. What would have been the effect on history if he had not lied to his father, and if Esau had had his rightful blessing? Jacob has also the distinction of being one of the world's first actors — all liars are of necessity actors — for did he not deceive his old father when he played his brother's part?

It is startling to note that some of the greatest lies — the lies that are quoted from generation to generation — have been the creations of the most honest men. Take, for instance, the extravagant ad-

ventures of Gargantua and Pantagruel, from the
pen of that doughty genius, Master François Rabelais.
The origin of his fabulous chronicles is interesting.
Gargantua first saw the light of day in a little sixteen-
page pamphlet issued in 1532 by Rabelais at Lyons,
where at that time he was a doctor at the Hôtel Dieu
on a salary of forty livres a year. To find this 'first'
of Gargantua is the hope of every book-collector.
For years the only copy known was safely locked up
in the Bibliothèque Nationale of Paris. It is imperfect, lacking a single leaf. Then, to the joy of many
noted bibliomaniacs, a complete copy was discovered
some years ago by Seymour de Ricci in the Munich
Library. How many years it had been there, while
all the bookstalls of Europe were searched in vain, or
how it got there, no one knew. But Rabelais' second
volume containing the adventures of Pantagruel, is
unique, and one of the treasures of the old Royal Library in Dresden. The combined stories of Gargantua
and Pantagruel appeared in Lyons in 1542; exactly
one dozen copies of this first edition have been found.
They are *introuvable*. In 1545, Rabelais edited a
third book, and in 1548, the fourth. The fifth, and
final book, only appeared in 1564, eleven years after
the author's death.

The adventures of the famous Grandgousier, his
gigantic son Gargantua, and his elephantine grandson Pantagruel have never had their equal in all
literature. In Rabelaisian parlance they are waggish,
whimsical, weird, exotic, egregious, eccentric, maca-
ronic, fantastic, farcical, flamboyant, brain-fuddling,

bombastic, bizarre, dissolute, droll, outlandish, thundering, and thumping.

Everyone knows the story of Gargantua's birth through his mother's ear, and how Gargantua in his turn, at 'the age of four hundred four score and four years, begat his son Pantagruel'! The lies contained in these marvelous histories are *living lies;* they will be quoted with gusto as long as man exists. No greater tribute can be paid to Rabelais.

But some men have unjustly acquired the reputation of being liars. It's a human trait to suspect the fellow who tells all.

Benvenuto Cellini falls into this class. His 'Autobiography' is often so startling that some scholars have believed this work to be purely fictitious. Cellini began it in 1558, when he was fifty-five, and ended it eight years later. Filled with bizarre experiences of every possible nature — murder, rape, robbery (and treason thrown in for good measure) — his autobiography has been placed among fictitious narratives.

Cellini says that 'All men who have done anything of excellence ought, if they are persons of truth and honesty, to describe their lives with their own hand.' You see, he esteemed himself an exponent of Truth. He considered himself strictly veracious. Exaggeration is the only thing that can be held against him.

I have always had the greatest affection for Cellini. It is a passion with me to secure autograph letters of my favorite characters, but where could I obtain one of Cellini's? One day in 1895, I was reading the catalogue of the collection of autograph letters owned by Alfred Morrison, and ran upon two of Cellini's. Immediately I longed to possess them. In 1917, when Mr. Morrison died, his collection was sold in London. Now was my chance! The Great War was on and there were few bidders. Even so, I was amazed to secure them for a comparatively small sum.

Now for my story. The most famous chapter in Cellini's autobiography tells of the casting in bronze of the great statue of 'Perseus Holding the Head of Medusa.'

To quote from the autobiography:

All of a sudden an explosion took place, attended by a tremendous flash of flame, as though a thunderbolt had formed and been discharged amongst us. Unwonted and appalling terror astonished everyone and me more even than the rest. When the din was over and the dazzling light extinguished, we began to look each other in the face. Then I discovered that the cap of the furnace had blown up, and the bronze was bubbling over from its source beneath. So I had the mouths of my mould immediately opened, and at the same time drove in the two plugs which kept back the molten metal. But I noticed that it did not flow as rapidly as usual, the reason being probably, that the fierce heat of the fire we kindled had consumed its base alloy. Accordingly I sent for all my pewter platters, porringers, and dishes, *to the number of some two hundred pieces*, and had a portion of them cast, one by one, into the channels, the rest into the furnace. This expedient succeeded and everyone could now perceive that my bronze was in most perfect liquefaction, and my mould was filling; where-

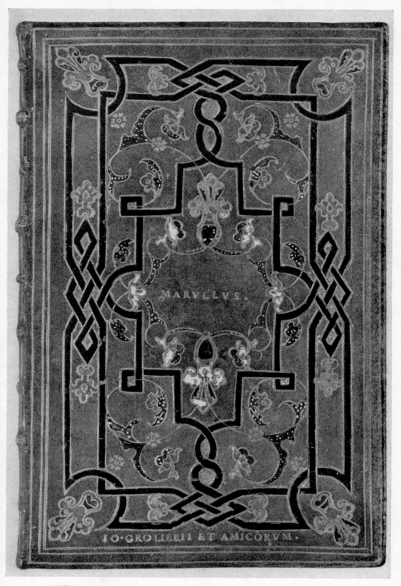

THE ONLY PERFECT INLAID GROLIER BINDING KNOWN

upon they all with heartiness and happy cheer assisted and obeyed my bidding, while I, now here, now there, gave orders, helped with my own hands, and cried aloud, 'O God! Thou that by Thy immeasurable power didst ascend to Heaven!' . . . even thus in a moment my mould was filled; and seeing my work finished, I fell upon my knees, and with all my heart gave thanks to God.

This celebrated passage, after innumerable readings, was photographed upon my memory. I awaited with anxiety the receipt of my two letters. On their arrival I read almost breathlessly Cellini's account, in his own handwriting, of the casting of the Perseus. At once I knew it was different from the published statement in his autobiography. It contained facts not hitherto known of the history of one of the world's most famous masterpieces. One of the letters, dated December 16, 1549, was entitled 'Account of Expenses incurred for the casting of Perseus.' It was addressed to Pier Francesco Ricci, Major-domo to Cosimo de Medici, Grand Duke of Tuscany, for whom the statue was made. It reads (in part) as follows:

On the 15th day of September 1549 we began to prepare the props for the casting of the Perseus with three structures; Master Bartolomeo, the smith, helped us with two of his workmen, and I leave out of reckoning three workmen of my own shop named Bernardino, Pietro, and Marchionne. We worked altogether up to the end of October, and I gave to the said Master Bartolomeo, for him and his two workmen at three lire and a half per day, twenty three ducates.

Also for 150 pounds of iron in two long bars which
we procured from Mr. Bindo Altoviti, as it was old
and good iron, which I used for Perseus, and after-
wards, as it can still be seen, for the furnace; at ten
lire the hundred pounds it amounts to

Also for three days' work to prepare for furnace and
in melting, to several men strong and suitable to this
great undertaking I paid thirteen ducats.

Also a load and two-thirds of elder wood bought of
Mr. Alessandro during the melting, for which I paid
four ducats.

Also a load of oak wood bought under the same circumstances of Mrs. Ginevra Del Capretta for seventeen lire.

Also for *22 pieces* of English pewter, namely, large
and middle-sized plates, seven of which were thrown
into the furnace on my becoming aware after the re-
moval of the tap that the metal flowed into the mould
irregularly owing to the unlucky accidents we met
with; the pewter cost me three ducats.

If you have read with care this long (and to me
fascinating) letter, you will notice that Cellini mentions twenty-two pieces of pewter that he threw into
the furnace. According to his autobiography he cast
into the flames *two hundred!* When writing his
memoirs, years after, his memory, to put it gently,
must have 'slipped.' The letter was penned about
sixteen years before his autobiography, so there is
some excuse for the lapse. At any rate, Cellini was
no liar, and we can only accuse him of a slight exaggeration. Today these precious letters may be read
in the Pierpont Morgan Library in New York City.

It must be said reluctantly that there is no love

Altera nunc rerum facies, me quero; nec adsum
Non sum qui fueram non putor esse: fui.

JACQUES CASANOVA DE SEINGALT
à l'âge de 63 ans

interest in these mighty books of lies. Well, gentle reader, I hear you ask, what about Casanova? Giovanni Jacopo Casanova de Seingault was but another truthful *raconteur!* And when he wrote in his memoirs that he did thus and so on a certain date; that he became a journalist, a preacher, an abbé, or a diplomat; that he gambled, cheated, lived by his wits at the expense of wealthy fools; that he fell in love, in debt, and in jail, you may rest assured you are reading the truth. There actually exist many old European court records, and a surprising number of inn registers and jail dockets, which bear Casanova's name, to prove and trace his checkered life. Many noted scholars, fascinated by the story of this *homme à bonnes fortunes*, have taken particular delight in keeping tabs on his spicy statements. They are eternally surprised by the fellow's extraordinary adherence to facts. Some I find difficult to credit, in spite of proof. My friend Seymour de Ricci has written a charming essay on Casanova which was privately printed for the Philobiblon Club, Philadelphia, 1923. I filch from it the story of Charpillon, the beautiful Swiss girl whose beauty was only surpassed by her wickedness. She fleeced Casanova unmercifully in London. He was furious and confesses that he made a fool of himself.

But he took his revenge. And it was unique. He bought a young parrot and spent a fortnight teaching it to repeat all day long: 'Charpillon is a bigger whore than her mother.' When he felt certain the bird had learned the statement, he sent it to the bird-market. Two days later all London flocked there to see and hear this wonderful bird. The two ladies thought of bringing an action for slander — but were perplexed — for how could one sue a bird?

The twelve bundles of Casanova's adventures, exactly as he wrote them, have never been issued completely. In 1820, over twenty years after Casanova's death, an Italian, Carlo Angiolini, brought the manuscript to the Leipzig publisher Brockhaus, who read it and was immediately shocked. But, as so often happens, he was fascinated, too. After due consideration he hired a German hack writer, Wilhelm Schutz, to excerpt and translate certain parts of Casanova's Italianized French. The result was bad — the exploits set down in a very poor German. Next, Aubry de Vitry re-translated the book into an equally poor French, and it was put on sale in France. Although obviously a translation of a translation, the memoirs caused great excitement and quickly became, in fact, a sensation.

> MUNCHAUSEN, BARON
>   Narrative of his Marvellous Travels
>   Oxford, 1786
>   12 mo, Calf.
>   First Edition — and Damn Rare!

This brief notice of the world's most glorious book of lies appeared in one of my recent catalogues. Orders for it poured in from all parts of the world. I felt like ordering it myself! The lucky man was Frank J. Hogan. I thought I had the first issue in

FRANK J. HOGAN

my private library in Philadelphia, but I was sadly mistaken. Mr. Hogan told me he wired for it more on account of the solitary 'damn' than for its rank among the great first editions. He thinks differently now.

In the *Critical Revue*, for December, 1785, there ran an abbreviated review of the first appearance of Baron Munchausen on this dismal planet, which he was to enliven so delightfully.

> This is a satirical production calculated to throw ridicule on the bold assertions of some parliamentary declaimers. If rant may be best foiled at its own weapons, the author's design is not ill-founded; for the marvelous has never been carried to a more whimsical and ludicrous extent.

On account of the date of this notice many students have come to the conclusion that the first edition of the Baron's quaint memoirs should be dated 1785. I doubt this very much. All copies that have turned up, and they have been few, bear the date 1786. It probably was printed late in the previous year, and only a few copies circulated.

The first issue was the one secured by Mr. Hogan. A little volume of forty-nine pages, it originally sold for a shilling. It was printed for Mr. Smith at Oxford, who turned out another edition in a few months' time (April). I have a copy of this second issue which contains 'Preface to the First Edition.'

> Baron Munikhouson, or Munchausen, of Bodenwerder, near Hameln on the Weser, belongs to the noble family of that name, which gave to the king's

German dominions the late prime minister, and several other public characters equally illustrious. He is a man of great original humour; and having found that prejudiced minds cannot be reasoned into common sense, and that bold assertors are very apt to bully their audience out of it; he never argues with either of them, but adroitly turns the conversation upon indifferent topics, and then tells a story of his travels, campaigns, and sporting adventures, in a manner peculiar to himself, and well calculated to awaken and put to shame the practice of lying, or, as it is politely called, drawing the long Bow.

As this method has been often attended with good success, we beg leave to lay some of the stories before the Public, and request those who fall into the company of notorious bouncers to exercise the same upon every proper occasion, i.e. where people seriously advance the most notorious falshoods under an appearance of truth, thereby injuring their own reputation, and deceiving those who are so unfortunate as to be in their hearing.

This April issue has also an extremely interesting 'Advertisement to the Second Edition':

The rapid demand for the first edition of this little pamphlet is a proof that the Public have seen it's moral tendency in a proper light: perhaps it should have been called with more propriety

The LYAR's MONITOR,

no vice is more contemptible than a habit of abusing the ears of our friends with falshoods.

The Baron is himself a man of great honor, and takes delight in exposing those who are addicted to deceptions of every kind, which he does with great pleasantry by relating the stories in large companies now presented to the Public in this little collection, which

BARON MUNCHAUSEN's
NARRATIVE

OF HIS

MARVELLOUS TRAVELS

AND

CAMPAIGNS

IN

RUSSIA.

HUMBLY DEDICATED AND RECOMMENDED

TO

COUNTRY GENTLEMEN;

AND, IF THEY PLEASE,

TO BE REPEATED AS THEIR OWN, AFTER A HUNT AT HORSE RACES, IN WATERING-PLACES, AND OTHER SUCH POLITE ASSEMBLIES; ROUND THE BOTTLE AND FIRE-SIDE.

OXFORD:

Printed for the EDITOR, and fold by the Bookfellers there and at Cambridge, alfo in London by the Bookfellers of Piccadilly, the Royal Exchange, and M. SMITH, at No. 46, in Fleet-ftreet.—And in Dublin by P. BYRNE, No. 108, Grafton-ftreet.

MDCCLXXXVI.

FIRST ISSUE OF BARON MUNCHAUSEN'S TRAVELS (*enlarged*)

is considerably enriched by his Naval or Sea Adventures, and also embellished with four Views from his own pencil.

London, April 20, 1786.

After the first two issues the publication rights were sold by Smith to G. Kearsley, of No. 46 Fleet Street, Oxford, who printed the third impression, containing five folding copper-plates. Its title was changed to

GULLIVER REVIVED;
Or the Singular
Travels, Campaigns, Voyages,
and Adventures
of
Baron Munikhouson,
commonly called
Munchausen:
The Third Edition, considerably enlarged, and ornamented with a number of Views engraved from the Original Designs.

It contains a notice as follows:

The Second impression was disposed of with such rapidity that a THIRD EDITION became necessary within three Weeks of the appearance of the former.

The additions are so considerable, both with respect to the Narrative and the Plates that it may fairly be considered as a new Work.

In the preface to Gulliver's Travels, which is a fine piece of irony, me (sic.) find the following passage.

'There is an air of truth apparent through the 'whole of these travels; and indeed the author

'was so distinguished for the veracity that it be-
'came a sort of proverb among his neighbours
'when any one affirmed a thing it was as true as
'if Mr. Gulliver had spoke it.'

The Editor of these adventures humbly hopes, they
will also be received with the same marks of respect,
and the exclamation of THAT'S A MUNCHAUSEN
given hereafter to every article of authentic intelligence.

May 18th, 1786.

In 1792 appeared from the press of H. D. Symonds,
Pater-noster Row, London, a worthless imitation,
but with twenty fascinating illustrations, including
a portrait of the famous Baron. It was entitled 'A
Sequel to the Adventures of Baron Munchausen,'
and was 'humbly dedicated to Mr. Bruce, The
Abyssinian Traveller.'

The Baron's adventures took London by storm.
The book created a stir on the Continent as well.
Everyone wondered who and where the author
was.

Baron Munchausen was a real person. But he
wasn't the author of the book. A cavalry officer,
Hieronymus Karl Friedrich, Freiherr von Munchausen, was in retirement at Bodenwerder in Hanover. Loquacious, genial, and loving an audience,
he frequented the beer-gardens and wine-cellars,
where he found plenty of company. He had really
seen service in Russia, and had also fought against the
Turks. It was his pleasure, over a stein of beer, or
glass of wine, to tell of his many extraordinary ex-

THE SINGULAR

TRAVELS, CAMPAIGNS, VOYAGES, and SPORTING ADVENTURES

OF

BARON MUNNIKHOUSON,

COMMONLY PRONOUNCED

MUNCHAUSEN:

As he relates them over a BOTTLE, when surrounded by his FRIENDS.

———————

A NEW EDITION, confiderably enlarged, and ornamented with four Views, engraved from the BARON's Drawings.

———————

OXFORD:

Printed and fold by the BOOKSELLERS of that UNIVERSITY, and at CAMBRIDGE, BATH and BRISTOL; in LONDON by M. SMITH, at No. 46, FLEET-STREET, and by the BOOK-SELLERS in PATER-NOSTER-ROW.

M DCC LXXXVI.

SECOND ISSUE OF BARON MUNCHAUSEN'S TRAVELS (*enlarged*)

ploits and to add, as his own, the martial triumphs
of others! A small group of admirers listened to this
loquacious fellow. His prowess as a soldier and
sportsman became a byword. A member of the
Baron's audience was a German writer named Rudolph Erich Raspe. Fascinated, Raspe joined the
company night after night, until he knew the stories
by heart.

It has always seemed to me strange that Rudolph
Erich Raspe, merely a chance listener, should
have been the first man to give the tales of Munchausen to the world. Raspe himself had a spectacu-
lar career. A scholar, noted at the Universities of
Leipzig and Göttingen, and connected with the
University library at Hanover, he was also Professor
of Archaeology at the Carolinium in Kassel. A gifted
gentleman was Raspe. When a valuable collection
of coins was placed in his care by the Landgrave of
Hesse — he was an antiquary — Raspe turned thief,
and sold many of the valuable medals entrusted to his
care. Arrested, he managed to escape, and eventually
turned up in England, an adventurer and an intellectual outcast.

In Scotland he swindled an employer, this time by
pretending to discover minerals in the ground which
he had placed there himself. When this swindle
was discovered, he disappeared once more, and little was known of him until his death in Ireland in
1794.

Not until he was down and out in London did Raspe
write the Baron's wild tales. Hoping to realize a few

shillings, he wrote the stories and doubtless felt lucky when he found a market for them. A peculiar mixture of scholar and rogue, Raspe's reputation has been kept alive, not by his serious literary labors, but by this work which he probably wrote at the instigation of an empty stomach.

The most wonderful and imaginative of all the Baron's original stories, the most realistic and sublimely ridiculous, I have always thought, is the one in which he tells of his 'superb Lithuanian horse,' which so often, so miraculously, carried him foremost into battle. Each of the many publishers of Munchausen has invariably had the good judgment to let this story remain. In this particular military pursuit the Baron, upon entering the market-place of a town, walked his panting charger to the spring to let him drink, where, according to him, the animal drank with an eagerness not to be satisfied. After a time the Baron, perched upon his back, happened to look around.

'What should I see, gentlemen?' he asks — 'the hind part of the poor creature, croup and legs were missing, as if he had been cut in two, and the water run out as it came in, without either refreshing him or doing him any good.' Mystified, but without explaining how he returns upon only the front half of his steed to the town gate, he continues, 'There I saw that when I rushed pell-mell with the flying enemy, they had dropt the port-cullis, unperceived by me, which had totally cut off his hind part, that lay still quivering on the outside of the gate. It would have been an irreparable loss, had not our own farrier contrived to bring both parts together while hot. He sewed them up with sprigs and young shoots of laurels that were just at hand — the wound healed, and what could not have happened but to so glorious a horse, the sprigs took root in his body, grew up, and formed a bower over me, so that afterward I could go upon many other expeditions in the shade of my own and my horse's laurels.' What modern liar can equal such graceful fantasy with so firm a foundation of lies that they seem to be the very truth?

Two years after the Munchausen stories were issued, Gottfried August Bürger, the German poet, foolishly published an edition in German at Göttingen, not far from the Baron's place of residence. Bürger carefully intimated that he had translated them from the English. No one knows how true this was, but the Baron and his friends seemed to recognize them as the Baron's own stories, word for word. He immediately started legal proceedings against Bürger, who changed the imprint from Göttingen to London. Even this did not appease the old fellow, and he harried him until he destroyed every unsold copy.

For nearly one hundred and fifty years the Munchausen stories have attracted all classes of society in all civilized countries. With the exception of 'Pilgrim's Progress,' 'Robinson Crusoe,' and 'Gulliver's Travels,' the 'Marvellous Travels of Baron Munchausen' has the distinction of being the most reprinted English book. It is now more popular than ever.

I had an amusing experience about two years ago. I was in a small town in Virginia, where I had gone to view a collection of Americana. I became so interested in the collection that I missed the one train that stopped daily en route North. The station-master remarked that a circus train was due to pass through. I knew the owner of the circus and immediately wired him for permission to travel along with the show some fifty miles to another station, where I could change to a regular passenger train. When the circus train arrived, I climbed into the car, curious as a little boy going to his first circus. But the elephants were at one end and the circus ladies elsewhere. It looked like a thoroughly boring trip — a circus train moves slowly — until the porter came along. He was an elderly, diminutive German, who sat himself down uninvited opposite me and began to talk. He was known to his circus friends as 'Shorty.' He regaled me with one of the most amazing collections of stories I have ever heard. He had caught an escaped circus tiger, the night before, he said, with his bare hands, and without assistance had replaced the animal in his cage; his sister owned a fifteen-carat diamond; his mother bore him when she was seventy-two; his father, ripe upon the bough at one hundred and two, was then dashing about the Riviera! As for him, he was working on the circus for the fun of the thing.

I listened, wide-eyed, and once, when he stopped to breathe, I exclaimed spontaneously, 'Why, you're a regular Baron Munchausen!'

He stopped and looked at me. 'How did you know?' he whispered. It was evident he had never heard of Munchausen. Flattered, he believed I thought him a German aristocrat traveling incognito. Immediately, I saw I had given him a new idea.

I understand this porter is still employed by the circus, but that his nickname has been changed from 'Shorty' to 'Baron,' and that I have become a legendary figure to whom he has sold his priceless collection of books!

Munchausen was an engaging villain who enjoyed telling his stories as much as his hearers enjoyed listening to them. There is nothing engaging about a literary faker of a slightly earlier period, George Psalmanazar, who, nevertheless, became one of the sensations of England. Unlike the Baron, he had no sense of humor, and his only object in perpetrating his stories seems to have been vanity and a love of notoriety. His real name has never been known. Psalmanazar he took from Shalmaneser in the second Book of Kings. At one time he held a passport where he was described as an Irish student, but he was probably a Frenchman. It was as a Formosan that he became known to fame. He was only twenty years of age when he gulled the British public with his 'Historical and Geographical Description of Formosa,' published in 1704. A second edition appeared in 1705. He even invented a Formosan language!

Doctor Johnson was taken in by him, and describes how, although he 'never sought much after anybody,' he 'sought after George Psalmanazar the most. I used to go and sit with him at an alehouse in the city.' The clergyman Innes, in order to help the fraud, pretended to convert him to Christianity and baptized him. For this noble action Innes received the appointment of chaplain-general to the English forces in Portugal!

Psalmanazar's 'Memoirs,' in which he exposed the fraud, were published posthumously in 1764. Psalmanazar's grandfather, if his grandson may be believed, lived to be one hundred and seventeen years of age, keeping his vigor by sucking every morning the blood of a viper! He would not have died so young, adds George, if they had not been forced to kill him!

Before I tell the story that follows, I have a confession to make. I must say that I take a perverse delight in adding to my private collection books so rare that they have survived in a single example. By this I do not mean trifles, but volumes of importance in the world of letters. It was with impish pleasure that I placed on the shelves, I hope never to depart, such appealing curiosities as the unique first edition of that interesting early 'Interlude for Children to play "Jack Juggler,"' 1560; the only example of that favorite of collectors, Nicolas Breton, the volume containing his finest poetry, 'The Passionate Shepherd,' 1604; the sole surviving 'History of Tom Thumb,' 1621; and the only perfect copy of that famous little anthology known as 'Davison's

Poetical Rhapsodie,' 1602. I must say I would hate
to see another of any one of these turn up! It is with
malicious interest that I show to my Elizabethan
and Jacobean friends these volumes that had the
stamina to resist the ceaseless wear of the ages, while
others of their fellows fell by the wayside.

What a horrible confession! Yes, I fear it is, but
what collector can resist the terrible appeal in an
auctioneer's catalogue, 'the only copy known'?
However, I am not quite so bad as it first appears, as
I am always glad to have scholars make use of my
unique volumes. Thus, my friend Hyder Rollins
has ably edited the 'Poetical Rhapsodie' for Harvard
College, and the learned Doctor W. W. Greg, of
University College, London, has given to the world,
with excellent notes, the 'Interlude of Jack Juggler.'

There was another collector with tastes similar to
my own, but who far surpassed my efforts in this
baleful pursuit. Needless to say he was a man after
my own heart. If he found that a certain volume he
treasured was no longer in the category of unique
volumes, he would dismiss it from his library with
a curse!

The gentleman was Jean-Nepomucène-Auguste
Pichauld, Count of Fortsas. From the exact in-
formation we now possess, we know he was born at
the Château de Fortsas, near Binche in Hainault
(Belgium), on October 24, 1770, and died there on
September 1, 1839.

For more than forty years the Count had such a
passion for the rarest volumes that it amounted to

frenzy. Never in the history of bookselling had there been such a sensational catalogue as the one of his library issued at Mons by Em. Hoyois in 1840, nearly a year after his death. In the 'Catalogue d'une très-riche mais peu nombreuse Collection de Livres provenant de la Bibliothèque de feu M. le Comte J.-N.-A. de Fortsas,' it was announced that the sale was to take place at Binche, on August 10, 1840, at eleven o'clock in the morning and under the direction and at the house of Monsieur Mourlon, notary, rue de l'Église, No. 9. A foreword to the catalogue, which is now itself a collector's item, contained interesting particulars as to the Count's method in forming his collection:

> The Count of Fortsas only made room upon his shelves for such works as were absolutely unknown to bibliographers and cataloguers; this was his rule and one from which he never departed. It will be readily believed that the collection made by him, and to which for forty years he devoted large sums of money, cannot possibly be numerous.
>
> It is still more difficult to believe that he ruthlessly expelled from his bookcases volumes for which he had paid their weight in gold as soon as he discovered that any work, till then supposed to be unknown, had been entered in any catalogue. Such works would have been as the apple of the eye to the most exacting amateur. A discovery so untoward would be indicated in his manuscript list, in a special column, by the words *Mentioned in such or such a work*, and then followed the expression *sold, given away*, or (an incredible thing unless one realizes how far the passion of an exclusive collector can go) *destroyed*.

CATALOGUE

D'UNE TRÈS-RICHE MAIS PEU NOMBREUSE COLLECTION

DE LIVRES

PROVENANT DE LA BIBLIOTHÈQUE

de feu M.ʳ le Comte J.-N.-A. DE FORTSAS,

dont la vente se fera à Binche, le 10 août 1840, à onze heures du
matin, en l'étude et par le ministère de M.ᵉ MOURLON, Notaire,
rue de l'Église, n.º 9.

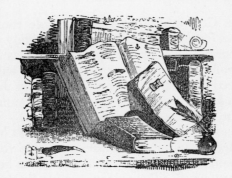

MONS.

TYPOGRAPHIE D'EM. HOYOIS, LIBRAIRE.

Prix : 50 Centimes.

TITLE-PAGE OF THE DE FORTSAS CATALOGUE, 1840

The publication of Brunet's 'Nouvelles Recherches' was a genuine blow to our bibliomaniac; one which could not fail to hasten his end. At one fell stroke a third of his library was wiped out. Afterward he appeared to be disgusted with books, and even with life itself. He did not acquire a single fresh volume. Techener's Bulletin issued from time to time thinned further the ranks of his already depleted collection.

The catalogue of the Fortsas library contained rather meager descriptions of only fifty-two books, for a thorough weeding-out had been done by the unfortunate and disappointed Count. Twelve pages out of the sixteen of the catalogue are devoted to an account of these books, the numbering from 3 to 222 being irregular, showing the interruption in the series when the Count decided to expel from his shelves a guilty volume.

The Fortsas sale took the bibliographical world by storm. Never before had there been so many rarities offered at one time, and every volume unique! When the bibliophiles received the catalogues from the little town of Mons, they almost went into convulsions. There were precious items in it that would make the most astute collector go wild to obtain; the Count seemed to possess an uncanny knowledge of what the bibliophile most desired in the secret places of his heart. There were scandalous chronicles of glamorous historical personages that were sure to make their descendants blush with shame. There was a witty but impudent libel entitled 'Les Suites du Plaisir, ou desconfiture du Grand Roi dans les Pais-

Bas. Au Ponent (Hollande) 1686,' bound in black morocco, tooled in gold, with a curious and daring plate. Another 'Aventures galantes du Captain Blainville' was printed at Brussels in 1746. There was a particularly naughty volume on the love-affairs of Prince Charles de Lorraine with Madame de Choiseul. A few historical works on the local histories of Rheims, Brabant, Hainault, and Binche further illumined the catalogue. There was only one work in English: 'Specimens of Early Flemish Songs of the Fourteenth Century to which is Prefixed an historical introduction by Georg. Ellis, Esq., Lond., 1809.'

Letters and commissions for certain items deluged the auctioneer. One noble lady, the Princess de Ligne, gave an unlimited order on one item which reflected on her illustrious grandfather. As the day of the sale drew near, the excitement increased. Brunet, the famous author of the 'Manuel du Libraire,' a book which the poor Count particularly detested, was almost in a fever to examine the books he had omitted from his great work. Renouard, the Aldine expert; Willems, the authority on the Elzevirs; the learned Baron de Reiffenberg, Director of the Royal Library at Brussels; and Techener, the well-known publisher and bookseller, whose monthly list almost drove the heartbroken Count mad, were all awaiting the fatal day. Other great amateurs, such as Joseph Octave Delapierre, Polain, and the mighty Charles Nodier, each hurried to Binche to steal a march on his fellows.

It was long before the days of motors and aeroplanes, and means of conveyance were not so plentiful as today. Consequently and quite naturally each bibliomaniac, in the final stage of the journey, found himself in the same coach with his competitor. Brunet, Nodier, Techener, and Renouard, once friends, now sat and glowered at each other in an enforced and unwelcome proximity until the painful journey came to an end. I know that feeling!

The worthy citizens of Binche must have looked with a curious and perhaps unfavorable eye on the influx of strangers on that tenth day of August, 1840. They seemed like inhabitants of another planet, chattering of imprints, title-pages, first editions, *moroquin citron*, and uncut edges!

They all asked about the eminent M. le Comte de Fortsas. The citizens silently shook their heads. And his famous château, where he was born and died? Silence was their only answer. M. Mourlon, the auctioneer and notary, of 9 Rue de l'Église, was quite unknown to these honest people.

A rumor reached the ears of the envious book-lovers that the town of Binche had purchased privately the Count's library in order to preserve intact his unique collection. This was denied by the town authorities who had no funds for such trifles! A sickly smile appeared on the face of each bibliophile. The bubble had burst.

You can imagine the chagrin of the book-world when it was discovered that it had been painfully deceived, that there was no count, no château, no notary Mourlon, no collection of unique volumes.

No wonder the natives of Binche called their strange visitors 'bibliofools.'

In time it came out that the whole affair was the invention of M. Renier H. G. Chalon, of Brussels, a well-known antiquarian and a member of the Royal Numismatic Society. Chalon's pleasant little jest was considered cruel by the 'expectant' collectors of his day. For a numismatist he had an extraordinary knowledge of books as the Fortsas catalogue shows. By this gay adventure he will live in the hearts of all bibliophiles.

It is with shame, and also pride, that I have to admit that the greatest of all literary hoaxes was a book-sale catalogue!

There are two famous lies that are inextricably connected with American history. The first is that of Captain John Smith and Pocahontas. This romantic incident, according to Captain Smith himself, occurred in December, 1607. The first appearance of this story in print is in the original edition of his 'Generall Historie of Virginia,' printed in 1624. The famous passage reads:

> Having feasted him after their best barbarous manner they could, a long consultation was held, but the conclusion was, two great stones were brought before Powhatan: then as many as could layd hands on him, dragged him to them, and thereon laid his head, and being ready with their clubs, to beate out his braines, Pocahontas the kings dearest daughter, when no intreaty could prevaile, got his head in her armes, and

laid her owne upon his to save him from death: whereat the Emperor was contented he should live to make him hatchets, and her bells, beads and copper.

The main reason for doubting the story seems to be in the fact that no mention of the experience with Pocahontas is made in the detailed personal narrative written by Smith and published less than a year after the incident. The 'True Relation of Virginia,' of which four editions appeared in 1608, omits this touching scene.

In 1616, Pocahontas and her husband, John Rolfe, journeyed to England, where they were handsomely received by the Queen and Worshipful Company of Cordwainers. Which reminds me that I owned at one time the very copy of the 'Generall Historie' that Smith presented to the hosts of Pocahontas, the 'Cordwayners of Ye Cittie of London.' On one of the front pages is a long inscription in Smith's handwriting. It is the only example of his writing that is known. Smith in this lengthy inscription entreats the members of the Guild to give his History 'lodging in your Hall freelie to be perused forever'! This magnificent volume, which has the arms of King James on both covers, I secured from Sir George Holford. It is now in the Henry E. Huntington Library at San Marino, California where it may be perused forever!

Pocahontas, as the first convert of her tribe to Christianity, and the attractive daughter of the Emperor Powhatan, became very popular in England. She was fêted everywhere. It is feared that the temptation to star her as the heroine of his own narrative was a little too much for Captain Smith to withstand. Accordingly he embellished his 'Generall Historie of Virginia' — which, by the way, is probably the most entertaining book in the whole range of Americana — with a brilliant 'invention.' The story of Pocahontas lives with the fame of Smith. When writing his history of Virginia, Captain Smith probably had no idea that the tale he had woven with so much ingenuity would be responsible for his renown in later centuries. So wags the world. The important and truthful chronicle of the first settlement of Jamestown pales in significance with the legendary story of the Princess Pocahontas. And so it should!

The greatest lie in American history was the achievement of a clergyman. The Reverend Mason L. Weems (1759–1825), formerly rector of Mount Vernon Parish in Virginia, was responsible for a canard that is known to every schoolboy in the United States. A few months after the death of George Washington, early in the year 1800, there appeared for the first time a little pamphlet entitled 'The Memorable Actions of George Washington, General and Commander in Chief of the Armies of America. Printed by and for George Keatinge, no. 207 Market St. (Baltimore, 1800).' Weems had worked on the manuscript while Washington was alive, and he recognized that he had a good thing in this 'unusual' memoir. Thus, he writes on June 24, 1799 (Washington died on December 14, 1799):

I have nearly ready for the press a piece christened, or to be christened, 'The Beauties of Washington.' 'Tis artfully drawn up, enlivened with anecdotes, and in my humble opinion marvellously fitted, 'ad captandum gustom populi Americani!'

Later, on January 12, 1800, Weems writes to Mathew Carey, the Philadelphia publisher, as follows:

Washington, you know is gone! Millions are gaping to read something about him. I am very nearly primed & cocked for 'em. 6 months ago I got myself to collect anecdotes of him. You know I live conveniently for that work. My plan! I give his history sufficiently minute — I accompany him from his start, thro the French & Indian & British or Revolutionary wars, to the President's chair, to the throne in the hearts of 5,000,000 of people. I then go on to show that his unparalleled rise and elevation were owing to his Great Virtues.... Thus I hold up his great Virtues to the imitation of Our Youth. All this I have lined and enlivened with Anecdotes apropos interesting and Entertaining.

General Henry Lee, in a contemporary notice of this famous biography, states, 'The Author has treated this great subject with admirable success in a new way.' 'The way' wasn't so novel. Parson Weems took particular delight in manufacturing out of the whole cloth anecdotes of his hero.

The story of George Washington and the cherry tree appeared like a sparkling gem in his 'Life' of the Father of his Country in the so-called fifth edition of 1806. Weems says himself that this anecdote 'is too valuable to be lost and too true to be doubted.' Weems thus places himself at once among the Munchausens of all time. Like all good liars he does not take credit for it himself, but puts the onus for it on an excellent lady to whom he was indebted for it. I cannot refrain from giving this celebrated story as it appears in the early editions:

'When George,' said she, 'was about six years old, he was made the wealthy master of a *hatchet* of which, like most little boys, he was immoderately fond, and was constantly going about chopping every thing that came in his way. One day, in the garden, where he often amused himself hacking his mother's pea-sticks, he unluckily tried the edge of his hatchet on the body of a beautiful young English cherry-tree, which he barked so terribly, that I don't believe the tree ever got the better of it. The next morning the old gentleman finding out what had befallen his tree, which, by the by, was a great favourite, came into the house, and with much warmth asked for the mischievous author, declaring at the same time, that he would not have taken five guineas for his tree. Nobody could tell him anything about it. Presently George and his hatchet made their appearance. "*George*," said his father, "*do you know who killed that beautiful little cherry-tree yonder in the garden?*" This was a *tough question*; and George staggered under it for a moment; but quickly recovered himself: and looking at his father, with the sweet face of youth brightened with the inexpressible charm of all-conquering truth, he bravely cried out, "*I can't tell a lie, Pa; you know I can't tell a lie, I did cut it with my hatchet.*" — "*Run to my arms, you dearest boy,*" cried his father in transports, "*run to my arms; glad am I, George, that you killed my tree; for you have paid me for*

THE REV. MASON L. WEEMS.

Died – 1825

From a print in the possession of D. McN. Stauffer, M Inst. C.E.

it a thousand fold. Such an act of heroism in my son is more worth than a thousand trees, though blossomed with silver, and their fruits of purest gold."'

Of the first edition of Parson Weems's 'Life of Washington,' only three copies have survived, and only one is perfect. It thus ranks in rarity with the early issues of Rabelais and Munchausen. I have the edition printed in Georgetown in 1800, which some authorities now consider the first. There must have been nearly a hundred editions of it since its first publication! Many a father, doubtless with a knowing grin on his countenance, has told the story of the cherry tree to his son, and later it was included in almost every First Reader. It had a strong appeal to many rising Americans, and even Abraham Lincoln was known to enjoy reading of the many virtuous exploits of the exemplary George.

The strange antics of Parson Weems when marketing his book are just as entertaining as the biography itself. He became the most famous itinerant bookseller of his time and it is a pity he did not write his own life. I think it would make more interesting reading than his celebrated biography of Washington, and he would *not* have had to manufacture the anecdotes. The parson was known throughout the Eastern States and his actions always excited the admiration of the crowd. He had no hesitation in proclaiming his 'Life of Washington' to be as great as Plutarch's 'Lives'; he would mount on a soap-box, first preach and then play the violin, join in with rustic dances, and later offer the volume at a price anywhere from twelve and a half to fifty cents! According to one authority 'Weems wrote a pamphlet entitled "The Drunkard's Looking-glass," illustrated with rude wood-cuts. This pamphlet he sold wherever he traveled. He entered taverns, addressed the company usually assembled in such places, imitated the foolish acts of an intoxicated person, and then offered his pamphlets for sale. His mimicry of a drunken man was generally taken as good-natured fun.'

So Parson Weems and Captain John Smith go hand in hand through the immortal shades. They are the creators of two stories that are woven in the fabric of American history. We simply cannot do without them. The two lies they told are harmless, but they have added to the gaiety of nations and to the good-will of all mankind. Has Truth achieved more?

IX

EARLIEST CHRISTMAS BOOKS

WHAT an exceedingly pleasant task to gather books relating to Christmas, all the way from Wynkyn de Worde, the successor of Caxton, the first English printer, to Charles Dickens.

These books are surely the collector's darlings, for, like early children's books, they have the qualities that are dearest to his heart — rarity, and charm of subject.

In order to appreciate the earliest volumes about Christmas in England, it is necessary to know something of the ancient observation of the festival, for, according to Polydore Vergil, 'the English celebrated the festival of Christmas with plays, masques, and magnificent spectacles, together with games at dice and dancing which was as ancient as the year 1170, and not customary with other nations.'

Picture yourself in one of the great houses of England in the sixteenth century. You have passed through the stately portals, hung with holly and mistletoe. You are one of the jolly throng assembled from the length and breadth of Britain, about to take part in festivities which had been celebrated every year, with perhaps but little change, for centuries past. For even King Arthur, according to the

'Ballad of Sir Gawain,' which will ring familiarly in
your ears,

> ... a royal Christmas kept
> With mirth and princely cheare;
> To him repaired many a knight
> That came both farre and neare.

With the laughing, chattering crowd you hastened
to the lofty baronial hall, ablaze with its rush lights
and the welcome of the huge yule log crackling on
the enormous hearth. With your lordly sixteenth-
century appetite, in a day before dyspepsia was ever
heard of, you sniffed expectantly and darted anxious
looks toward the center of the room, where the dark
oak table stretched its mighty length. Old Thomas
Tusser tells us some of the good things one would
expect to find on it:

> Brawn, pudding and souse, and good mustard withal,
> Beef, mutton, and pork shred pies of the best,
> Pig, veal, goose, and capon and turkey well dressed,
> Cheese, apples, and nuts, jolly carols to hear,
> As then in the country is counted good cheer.

No wonder the board groaned!

By the way, it was Thomas Tusser who wrote
what are probably the two best-known lines on
Christmas:

> At Christmas play and make good cheer,
> For Christmas comes but once a year.

But where was the glorious boar's head all this
time, without which no Christmas feast would be
complete? Yonder it came, surrounded by baked

VIRGIN AND CHILD FROM A BOOK OF HOURS
ILLUMINATED BY NICHOLAS SPIERINCK

ANNUNCIATION FROM A BOOK OF HOURS
ILLUMINATED BY NICHOLAS SPIERINCK

apples whose bursting skins sent out little spouts of steam, and borne proudly aloft on its salver by the faithful steward. You recalled at once the text of the ancient half-Latin carol:

> Caput apri differo
> Reddens laudes domino.
>
> The bores heed in hand bring I
> With garlans gay and rosemary.
> I praye you all synge merely
>   Qui estis in conuiuio.
>
> The bores heed I understande
> Is the chefe seruyce in this lande
> Loke where euer it be fande
>   Seruite cum cantico.
>
> Be gladde lordes bothe more and lesse
> For this hath ordeyned our stewarde
> To chere you all this Christmasse
> The bores heed with mustarde.

The boar's head must have been a sight to behold, for

> If you would send up the brawner's head
> Sweet rosemary and bays around it spread;
> His foaming tusks let some large pippin grace,
> Or midst these thundering spears an orange place;
> Sauce like himself, offensive to his foes,
> The roguish mustard, dangerous to the nose,
> Sack and the well-spiced hippocras, the wine,
> Wassail, the bowl with ancient ribands fine,
> Porridge with plums, and turkeys with the chine.

After you had polished off all the food in sight, with your share of the 'wilde boare,' you still could smack your lips over 'plum puddings, pancakes, apple-pies and custard.' But perhaps you refused these, and waited for the mince-pies. These delicacies were a real part of Christmas, for they were baked in oblong form in remembrance of the manger at Bethlehem. The meat used in them was mutton, to represent the shepherds' flock; the spices were for the frankincense and myrrh, brought by the adoring Magi.

Mince-pie was so important to the Christmas feasting that later on, in the days of the Puritans, to eat or not to eat a mince-pie became a test of religious creed. It has been said, though I imagine without much truth, that it was his refusal to eat mince-pie that kept John Bunyan in prison, when he might otherwise have been released. If there is anything in the story, how much we are indebted to this delicacy, for without it the 'Pilgrim's Progress' might never have been written! The makers of mince-pies in early England 'had nothing on' our own florists at Mother's Day, for there is an old English superstition that as many mince-pies as you taste at Christmas so many happy months will you have. The mince-pies merchants thus were sure of at least twelve pies to every man, woman, and child in the kingdom!

And then the wassail bowl, with its hot spiced ale. At its advent the host rose up with the time-honored toast, the words of the carol: 'God rest you Merry, Gentlemen, let nothing you dismay!'

Suddenly, above the hubbub of the feast, rang clear upon the frosty night air the voices of the villagers, singing as they approached.

VIRGIN AND CHILD FROM A BOOK OF HOURS ILLUMINATED
BY GEOFFROY TORY

'The waits! The waits!' the guests shouted. For at that season men and boys dressed in 'antick' garb and went caroling from door to door the night through. The servants flung open the doors and bade them enter, and the merry crew began their round of song with:

Wassail and wassail all over the town,
The cup it is white and the ale it is brown;
The cup it is made of the gold old ashen tree,
And so is our beer of the best barley.
To you a wassail!
Aye, and joy come to our jolly wassail.

O maid, O maid, with your silver headed pin,
Pray open the door and let us all in,
All for to fill our wassail bowl and so away again
To you a wassail!
Aye, and joy come to our jolly wassail.

O maid, O maid, with your glove and your mace,
Pray come unto this door and show your pretty face,
For we are truly weary of standing in this place.
To you a wassail!
Aye, and joy come to our jolly wassail.

O master and mistress, if you are so well pleased
Pray set all on your table, your white bread and cheese
And put forth your roast beef, your porrops and your pies
To you a wassail!
Aye, and joy come to our jolly wassail.

O master and mistress, if we've done any harm,
Pray pull fast this door and let us pass along,
And give us hearty thanks for singing our song,
To you a wassail!
Aye, and joy come to our jolly wassail.

To know what ballads these revelers sang we must search through the popular literature of their day. Caxton himself most probably printed collections of them, though not even a fragment by him has survived.

Christmas has been termed the rarest feast of all — but not so rare, to play upon the word, as the little volumes of carols put out by the successors of Caxton: Wynkyn de Worde, William Copland, and others of the early sixteenth-century printers in England. However many copies of their carols these worthy men printed — and the number probably went into the hundreds, for they were peddled in the streets at Christmas time — only four small fragments now remain, each of the four being a portion of a separate edition. Three of these four, two of which are the merest fragments, are the prized possessions of the University of Oxford.

The earliest of these was printed by Wynkyn de Worde in 1521, and alas! only one leaf remains. It was entitled 'Christmasse carolles newely enprinted,' and the one surviving leaf contains the 'boar's head carol' I have already quoted. This is still sung on Christmas Day at some of the Oxford colleges, and according to a letter quoted by Dibdin from a Mr. Dickinson, tutor at Queen's in 1811, it is 'sung to the common chaunt of the prose version of the Psalms in Cathedrals.' The words as quoted by Mr. Dickinson differ slightly from the version I have printed.

William Copland and R. Jones also printed copies

of the same carols as Wynkyn de Worde and the single copy or fragment of each which has survived is also in the Bodleian Library.

The remaining one of the four early editions still extant, I am happy to say, is now in America, for I myself was lucky enough to win a brave fight for it with my English competitors at a session of the now historic Britwell Court Sales in London. It is now safely housed in the Huntington Library in California. It bears the same title as the others — 'Christmas Carolles newely inprynted,' and strange to say has a woodcut of the Crucifixion on the title-page, instead of the Nativity, which one would rather expect. It was 'Inprynted at London in the Powltry by Richard Kele, dwellyng at the longe shop under saynt Myldredes chyrche.' The date of this publication is not known, but it was certainly not later than 1546, for in that year Kele moved from the 'longe shop' and went to the Eagle in Lombard Street.

Let one of the early owners tell you why he preserved it. He has written his reason in front of the book.

This old Pamphlet was a part of a collection of Curiosities made by that famous Antiquary and Historian Mr. Roger Morrice late of Hoxton in the County of Middx deed. . . . Wherefore, it having been preserved thus long from the devouring Jaws of Time, I thought it to be valuable purely for its Antiquity; and have accordingly carefully lay'd it up & preserved it for about or near to 30 years, that it has been in my Hands. And that it may not be thrown away as an imperfect and good-for-nothing Piece after I am dead and gon (*sic*), is what is designed in my Writing of this Recommendation of it. Sam. Marriott. Octobr. 15, 1733.

Other carols and Christmas ballads, some with most enticing titles, we know were printed, but of them alas! no trace remains today. We have records of 'A christmas Warnynge for hym yt intendethe to Ryde and make mery abrode with his fryndes, A ballad,' 1567; 'A godly hymne or caroll for Christmas,' 1579; 'Godlie Carolles Hymnes and Spersall Songes,' 1580; 'A book of Carolles set forth by Moses Powell,' 1586; 'A new ballad intituled Christmas Delights,' 1593; and toward the end of the century 'Christmas Delights,' and 'The Praise of Christmas To the tune of "When Phœbus did rest." '

Possibly the earliest Christmas hymn ever written is the famous Nativity Hymn of Saint Ambrose, 'Veni Redemptor gentium' — 'Redeemer of the Nations, come' — which is still sung in the churches at Christmas time. The most popular and universally known of them all, the 'Adeste Fideles' — 'O come all ye faithful,' has been credited to Saint Bonaventura, but I imagine with little truth, and that it really dates from a later period.

One of the earliest English carols is supposed to have been composed by Dunstan, the famous abbot of historic Glastonbury in the tenth century. The story goes that the original manuscript was found among his papers after his death. Dunstan's carol is

of the favorite cumulative type. I expect you all
know it:

> Come and I will sing to you.
> What will you sing to me?
> I will sing you one-ery.
> What is your one-ery?
> One and one is all alone and ever more shall be so;

and so on, accumulating with each verse until twelve-
ery is reached. Twelve is, of course, the all-important
number at Christmas time, as the Christmas festivities lasted for twelve days until Twelfth Night.

The last verse of another famous cumulative carol,
probably dating from about the same period as
Abbot Dunstan's, reads,

> On the twelfth day of Christmas
>   my true love sent to me
> Twelve bells a-ringing
> Eleven bulls a-beating
> Ten asses racing
> Nine ladies dancing
> Eight boys a-singing
> Seven swans a-swimming
> Six geese a-laying
> Five goldie rings
> Four colley birds
> Three French hens
> Two turtle doves
> And the part of the mistletoe bough.

Carols and ballads were not the only form of fifteenth-century Christmas literature, and even the
old theologians tried their hand at some form of

Christmas composition. In 1542 Thomas Becon, a protestant divine, published 'A Christmas bankette' under his pseudonym of T. Basille, and a few years later he wrote 'A newe Dialoge betwene thangel of god and the Shepherds of ye felde, concerning the Nativitie and byrth of Jesus Christ our Lord and savior, no lesse godly than swete and pleasante to reade.'

The miracle and mystery plays of the thirteenth to the sixteenth centuries, which were performed at certain stated religious festivals of the year, Christmas being one, took their subjects from sacred history and the legends of the saints, and naturally included representations of the Nativity. The spirit and feeling of these religious plays was naïve and simple to a degree, in order to be within the comprehension of all, and was reminiscent of the spirit of the pictorial representations to be found in the illuminated missals and other service books of the same period, where the treatment is equally naïve.

In the missals, for example, the shepherds will frequently be found, in the appropriate costume of their country, expressing their joy at the news of the angels by dancing a folk-dance to music. In the mystery plays, the shepherds, similarly dressed in the native English costume of their calling, dance and show their pleasure by such homely expressions as 'We! hudde!'; 'We! howe!' (somewhat reminiscent of the 'And How!' of our own day); and 'We! colle!' now pronounced 'Oh golly!'

In the second Shepherd's Play in the Towneley

cycle, it is the shepherds who provide much of the comic element.

Mak, the sheep stealer, succeeds in snatching one of their sheep, and in order to conceal it, he and his wife place it in a cradle. On the arrival of the shepherds to search for their lost property, Mak pretends that the occupant of the cradle is a new-born baby. The shepherds' discovery of the sheep gives rise to much hilarity and merriment, and Mak is tossed in a blanket until they are all exhausted and lie down to sleep. They are awakened by an angel who tells them the news of the birth of the Saviour.

In striking contrast to the simplicity of the mystery plays is the rich pageantry of the Elizabethan Christmas spectacles. One has only to read the account by Dugdale, in the 'Origines Juridiciales,' of the magnificent Christmas entertainment at the Inner Temple in the fourth year of Queen Elizabeth's reign to realize how important the season of Christmas had become.

Many of the most famous dramatists of Elizabeth's reign wrote Christmas Masques for performance at the Court or the Temples. In the second volume of the 'Works of Ben Jonson,' 1640, can be found, for example, 'Christmas his Masque, as it was presented at Court.' It has always seemed strange to me that there is so little mention of Christmas throughout the works of Shakespeare.

Possibly the spirit of Christmas had little appeal for him, though on at least one occasion he mentions some of the traditional folk-lore connected with the festival. I am referring to the fact that the ghost of Hamlet's father vanished at cock-crow. You will remember that Marcellus explains:

> It faded on the crowing of the cock.
> Some say, that ever 'gainst that season comes
> Wherein our Saviour's birth is celebrated
> This bird of dawning singeth all night long:
> And then, they say, no spirit dares stir abroad.
> The nights are wholesome; then no planets strike,
> No fairy takes, nor witch hath power to charm,
> So hallow'd and so gracious is the time.

As a season of merriment Christmas is apparently only mentioned twice throughout his plays, and in each case the tone seems to be slightly disparaging. In the Induction to the 'Taming of the Shrew,' Sly gives his assent to the playing of the comedy by saying,

> 'Marry I will; let them play it: Is not a
> commonty a Christmas gambol, or a tumbling trick?'

The second reference is in 'Love's Labour's Lost,' where Biron's reply to the question of the Princess, 'Will you have me or your pearl again?' is:

> Neither of either; I remit both twain. —
> I see the trick on 't; — Here was a consent,
> (Knowing aforehand of our merriment)
> To dash it like a Christmas comedy.

Biron seems to have been fond of Christmas, for he also makes mention of the weather one should expect at this season:

> At Christmas I no more desire a rose
> Than wish a snow in May's new-fangle snow.

R. Mocrice

¶Christmas ca=
rolles newely Inprynted.

**¶ Inprynted at London in the Powl=
try by Rychard Kele , dwellyng at the
longe shop vnder saynt Myldre=
des chyrche,** ☙ ❧ ❧

CHRISTMAS CAROLS, LONDON, CIRCA 1546. THE ONLY COPY
KNOWN

Behold the maieſtie and grace——
of loueing, cheerfull, Chriſtmas face.
Whome many thouſands with one breath:
Cry out let him be put to death.
Who indeede Can neuer die:
So long as man hath memory.

'THE EXAMINATION AND TRYAL

THE

EXAMINATION

AND

TRYAL

of Old Father

CHRISTMAS;

Together with his Clearing by the
JURY,

At the Affizes held at the Town
of *Differenee*,' in the County of
Difcontent.

Written according to Legal Proceeding,
By *Jofiah King*.

Licenfed, *Aug.* 10. 1677. *Ro. L'Eftrange.*

London, Printed for *H. Brome, T. Baffet,*
and *J. Wright*. 1678.

Most of the writers of the seventeenth century held Christmas in the greatest esteem, and the festival was enriched by a number of magnificent poems, now included in collections of carols, but many of which were almost certainly meant to be read rather than sung. Ben Jonson, George Herbert, George Wither, Robert Southwell, Robert Herrick, John Milton — I can scarcely refrain from including Uncle Tom Cobleigh — all wrote magnificent Christmas carols.

It is not surprising to find the royalist Herrick writing his beautiful 'Star Song: a carrol to the King: sung at White-Hall.'

> Tell us, thou cleere and heavenly Tongue
> Where is the Babe but lately sprung?
> Liest he the Lillie-banks among?
>
> Or say, if this new Birth of ours
> Sleeps, laid within some Ark of Flowers
> Spangled with dew-light; thou canst cleere
> All doubts, and manifest the where
>
> Declare to us, bright Star, if we shall seek
> Him in the Mornings blushing cheek
> Or search the bed of Spices through,
>   To find him out?

Herrick wrote several beautiful carols, and also minor poems on the Christmas ceremonies:

> Come bring with a noise
> My merrie merrie boyes,
> The Christmas log to the firing
> While my good Dame, she
> Bids ye all be free
> And drink to your hearts desiring.

And again:

> Come guard this night the Christmas pie
> That the thiefe, though ne'er so slie,
>   With his Flesh-hooks don't come in
>   To catch it.

Herrick was an ardent royalist and a firm believer in celebrating Christmas time in the old-fashioned way. Milton, however, was a Puritan and that he should have written Christmas hymns is a matter of some surprise. All know his noble 'Hymn. On the Morning of Christ's Nativity':

> This is the month, and this the happy morn,
> Wherein the Son of Heaven's eternal King
> Of wedded maid and virgin mother born
> Our great redemption from above did bring
> For so the holy sages once did sing
> That he our deadly forfeit should release
> And with his Father work us a perpetual peace.

That December twenty-fifth should be referred to as a 'happy morn' by such a stern adherent of the Puritan principles is somewhat extraordinary, for after the death of the first King Charles all Christmas jollities were frowned upon, and Christmas celebrations fell on evil days. In 1644, the Long Parliament ordered that the twenty-fifth of December should be kept as a national fast, not feast, and that 'all men should pass it humbly bemoaning the great national sin which they and their fathers so often committed on that day by romping under the mistletoe, eating boar's head, and drinking ale flavored with roasted apples.'

Imagine the dissatisfaction and grumbling to which this decree gave rise! It resulted in much breaking of the law, naturally, and in much pamphlet literature.

In 1648, for instance, was published: 'Canterbury Christmas: or A True Relation of the Insurrection in Canterbury on Christmas Day last, with the great hurt that befell divers persons thereby, written by a Citizen there, to his friend in London.' This pamphlet gives an account of the subsequent proceedings after the 'Cryer' of Canterbury had upon Wednesday, December 22, 'by the appointment of Master Mayor, openly proclaimed that Christmas Day and all other superstitious festivals should be put downe, and that a Market should be kept on Christmas Day. Which being not observed (but very ill taken by the Country), the town was thereby unserved with provision and trading very much hindered; which occasioned great discontent among the people, caused them to rise in a rebellious way.'

Many such pamphlets must have been issued at the time, but very few have survived.

Among the rarest of these, as well as one of the most remarkable, is 'The Examination and Tryal of Old Father Christmas'; printed in London in 1678, after the re-establishment of Christmas festivities by Charles II. In this quaint little volume, written in the form of an allegory with a Bunyanesque flavor, 'one old Christmas was commanded to be brought to the Bar, then was a jury for Life and Death to be impaneled.' 'The Judge was called Hate-Bate, the Sheriff's name was called Leonard

Love-peace,' and so on, every name being allegor-
ically appropriate.

In the end, needless to say, Christmas is properly
and completely acquitted, but is cautioned by the
judge that, 'for avoiding all such scandals as have
been cast upon you, for the future, do think fit to
admonish you, that you remember your Office is not
so much to feast the Body, as to refresh the Soul, by
thankful and pious Meditations.' The 'jolly Old
Father Christmas' agreed to the terms imposed, and
has never been brought up for trial since!

The revival of the Christmas festivities after the
Restoration was celebrated in a ballad 'Old Christmas Returned.'

> All you that to feasting and mirth are inclined
> Come, here is good news for to pleasure your mind;
> Old Christmas is come for to keep open house,
> He scorns to be guilty of starving a mouse;
> Then come, boys, and welcome for diet the chief,
> Plum-pudding, goose, capon, minced pies and roast beef.

There are naturally very few Christmas books of
colonial American origin. The early settlers in this
country were for the most part Puritans who had left
their native land in order to be free from all religious
forms and ceremonies, and the majority of them ig-
nored Christmas as a festival. But the celebration of
Christ's birthday was not blotted out of the calendar
without a good deal of protest, particularly on the
part of the younger members of the Colony, who remembered with regret the good times they had had

at home. In William Bradford's 'History of Plimmouth Plantation' we read:

> On the day called Christmas day ye Governor called them out to work (as was usual), but the most of this new company excused themselves and said it went against their consciences to work on that day. So the Governor told them that if they made it a matter of conscience, he would spare them until they were better informed. So he led away the rest and left them. But when they came home at noon from their work, he found them in the street at play openly, some pitching the bar and some at stoole-ball and such like sports. So he went to them and took away their implements and told them it was against his conscience that they should play and others work.

In 1651, the Massachusetts Legislature went so far as to pass an act imposing a fine of five shillings upon 'whoever shall be found observing any such day as Christmas, or the like, either by forebearing labor, feasting, or any other way upon any such account.' This law was repealed in 1682, but even so there was so much feeling against the celebration of Christmas that there was no universal observance of December twenty-fifth as a feast-day in this country until the nineteenth century.

Christmas, therefore, meant very little to the children of the early settlers, and even as late as the nineteenth century their parents did not think it necessary to give them Christmas presents, or, if they did, they merely added insult to injury by giving them lesson-books in the guise of presents!

In my collection of early American children's

books, I find titles that make me feel truly sorry for the unfortunate youngsters. The German children would seem to have been the worst sufferers. I have, for example, two rare little books in German printed at New Market, Virginia, in 1809, one for boys and one for girls — 'Ein Christags-Geschenk für kleine Knaben' [or alternatively for 'kleine Mägdlein], oder eine Sammlung von verschiedenen Unterretungen.' One can imagine how annoyed a child of today would be at taking such a 'Geschenk' out of his stocking!

The early American children, however, had one 'break' — they could learn all about Christmas from some of the most delightful little books in the world, so delightful in fact that, although many editions were published, very few have survived and copies are now excessively rare. I am referring to 'The History of the Holy Jesus,' which tells the story of Christ in doggerel verse, and I am looking now at my copy of an edition printed in Boston in 1749. We can imagine the little Bostonians reading

> The Wise Men from the East do come,
> Led by a shining Star,
> And offer to the new-born King,
> Frankincense, Gold and Myrrh.
>
> Which Herod hears, and wrathful grows,
> And now by Heav'n's Decree
> Joseph and Mary and her Son
> Do into Egypt flee.
>
> The bloody Wretch, enrag'd to think
> Christ's death he could not gain,
> Commands that Infants all about
> Bethlehem should be slain,

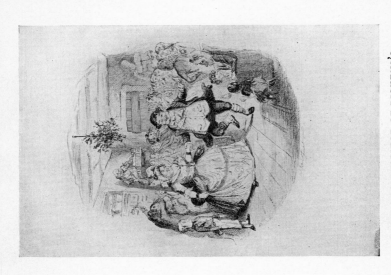

THE FRONTISPIECE OF DICKENS'S
'CHRISTMAS CAROL'

To Henry Austin from Charles Dickens

Devonshire Terrace
Friday Decr 22nd 1843

PREFACE.

I HAVE endeavoured in this Ghostly little book, to raise the Ghost of an Idea, which shall not put my readers out of humour with themselves, with each other, with the season, or with me. May it haunt their houses pleasantly, and no one wish to lay it.

Their faithful Friend and Servant,

C. D.

December, 1843.

PRESENTATION COPY OF DICKENS'S
'CHRISTMAS CAROL'

and then turning to gaze in wonder on the accompanying wood-cut illustrations. The picture of the Wise Men shows a group of Puritans gazing through a telescope at a shooting star, plainly visible in a sky thick with stars of all sizes. Turning over the page, they would then come to Herod slaying the 'Innocent Children.' This is, indeed, wonderful to behold, for the 'bloody Wretch' is depicted, fully armed, with sword in hand, dashing on a charger between two armies (one carrying the British flag!) with corpses of soldiers strewing the ground!

If, owing to the nature of things, there could be no Christmas literature amongst the early settlers in America, later American writers have certainly made up for the lack. Every English-speaking person the world over knows Clement C. Moore's

'Twas the night before Christmas, when all through the house
Not a creature was stirring — not even a mouse:

whose author's claim to immortality rests on this work alone, and not on his learned 'Compendious Lexicon of the Hebrew Language in Two Volumes.'

For a long time the authorship of this famous poem — whose real title is 'A Visit from St. Nicholas' — was unknown. Its first appearance in print was anonymous, in the *Troy Sentinel* for December 23, 1823, introduced by a blurb beginning, 'We know not to whom we are indebted for the following description of that unwearied patron of children — that homely and delightful personage of parental kindness —

Santa Claus . . .' It was reprinted by the same newspaper at Christmas time year after year and copied by other newspapers throughout the country. It was not until the issue of the *Troy Budget* for December 25, 1838, that the authorship was publicly acknowledged. In 1844, 'A Visit from St. Nicholas' was included in the collected poems of Clement C. Moore. Since then it has been reprinted countless times, and no anthology is complete without it.

According to one version of the origin of this poem, it was written on Christmas Eve in 1822. Mrs. Moore had sent her husband to buy an additional turkey needed for one of her Christmas baskets, and, returning with the bird under his arm, struck by the beauty of the night, and inspired with the spirit of Christmas, he determined to write a tribute to St. Nicholas as soon as he arrived home. The result was 'A Visit to St. Nicholas,' composed simply for the delight of his own children. The following year Miss Harriet Butler, a guest in the house, asked if she might make a copy and she it was who was apparently responsible for the subsequent appearance of the poem in the *Troy Sentinel*. This unauthorized appearance of his verses in print is said to have caused considerable annoyance to the good author, who did not realize at first that the poem written for the amusement of his own family was to be a source of joy to countless children down the ages.

Moore is one of many of the nineteenth-century Americans who have written Christmas songs and ballads. Longfellow, Whittier, Washington Irving,

Lowell, in fact all the great American writers, have celebrated Christmas in song.

I have devoted this chapter principally to Christmas as celebrated years ago in carol and song. For the most beautiful pictorial representations of the Nativity you must search the early missals, most of them executed long before the invention of printing. In these precious books the illustrations of the first Christmas are, as I have already mentioned, rendered with an appealing naïveté and charm not to be found elsewhere, and only to be paralleled in the dramatic representations of the same period.

One of the illustrations which we reproduce is one of the most beautiful of the fifteenth-century miniatures of the Nativity. The original is on parchment, exquisitely painted *en grisaille*, and delicately heightened with gold. The workmanship and artistry are perfect, and the miniature could have been produced only by a supreme master of his art. In the opinion of experts it is in all probability the work of the Master of Zwolle, a Flemish painter and engraver who lived in the latter half of the fifteenth century. The central picture depicts the scene at the Nativity. Joseph and the Virgin are kneeling in adoration of the Holy Babe, Who is lying, surrounded by golden rays, in the center of the stable on a truss of straw. On the right, descending in a burst of clouds, is a choir of over twenty angels singing the 'Gloria in Excelsis.' Forming a border about the left side and base of this large picture are nine smaller ones depicting scenes from the life of the Virgin and the childhood of Christ.

I will close with these lines from Whittier's 'Christmas Carmen' which seem particularly appropriate at the present time:

> Blow, bugles of battle, the marches of peace;
> East, west, north, and south let the long quarrel cease;
> Sing the song of great joy that the angels began,
> Sing the glory to God and of good-will to man!

THE END

Index

INDEX